Joseph Itiel is a graduate of the Training Division of the Hypnosis Clearing House in Oakland, California. In addition to his private practice in motivational hypnotherapy, he gives seminars, courses, and demonstrations for various San Francisco Bay Area colleges and organizations. He is certified by the California Hypnotists Examining Council and holds an M.A. degree from The City College of New York.

Financial Well-Being Through Self-Hypnosis

Joseph Itiel

A SPECTRUM BOOK

Prentice-Hall, Inc., Englewood Cliffs, N.J. 07632

Library of Congress Cataloging in Publication Data

Itiel, Joseph.

Financial well-being through self-hypnosis.

"A Spectrum Book."
Includes index.
1. Finance, Personal. 2. Hypnotism—Therapeutic use.
3. Self-actualization (Psychology) I. Title.
HG179.I85 1983 332.024 83-11097
ISBN 0-13-316489-6
ISBN 0-13-316471-3 (pbk.)

This book is available at a special discount when ordered in bulk quantities. Contact Prentice-Hall, Inc., General Publishing Division, Special Sales, Englewood Cliffs, N.J. 07632.

A Spectrum Book. Printed in the United States of America.

10 9 8 7 6 5 4 3 2 1

ISBN 0-13-316489-6

ISBN 0-13-316471-3 {PBK.}

Manufacturing buyer: Pat Mahoney

Prentice-Hall International, Inc., *London*
Prentice-Hall of Australia Pty. Limited, *Sydney*
Prentice-Hall Canada Inc., *Toronto*
Prentice-Hall of India Private Limited, *New Delhi*
Prentice-Hall of Japan, Inc., *Tokyo*
Prentice-Hall of Southeast Asia Pte. Ltd., *Singapore*
Whitehall Books Limited, *Wellington, New Zealand*
Editora Prentice-Hall do Brasil Ltda., *Rio de Janeiro*

CONTENTS

PREFACE

The purpose of this book is to help you gain better control over your financial destiny. After you have finished the book and have done the self-hypnosis exercises, you will be able to start shaping the three major areas that contribute to your financial well-being: your occupation, your material acquisitions, and your overall income.

The vehicle for accomplishing all this is visualization in a state of self-hypnosis. Hypnosis has been used traditionally in health-related areas such as weight control, smoking, and phobias. When linked with visualization, hypnosis is just as effective in exploring and setting goals. This work uses these techniques to help you explore your financial needs and wants and then bring about the changes that will harmonize the economic aspects of your life.

The advantage of this approach is that it is self-oriented, is easy to learn, and does not require major expenditures. (A cassette recorder and a few cassettes are all that you need.) It does involve a certain amount of work in getting started and in practicing the exercises. Because so much of the time you will be in a state of self-hypnosis, it will be a very relaxing experience.

The exercises are the heart of the book. You will derive the full benefit from them only if you *do* them. Reading them will result in intellectual benefits, but only on a conscious level. By recording and doing the exercises you will reap the benefits of being in touch with your subconscious mind.

Whether you believe or agree with the theories and opinions in this book has no bearing on your success with the exercises. Through them you will learn to converse with yourself so that the total "you" will be involved in shaping your financial affairs. You will shape them the way *you* want them, to suit *your* needs and aspirations.

When you have finished with the exercises, you will have learned how to hypnotize yourself simply by having done it successfully a number of times. I have included a chapter on how to formulate posthypnotic suggestions and affirmations correctly. This will allow you to use self-hypnosis as a tool to enhance the quality of your life in whatever area you choose.

You probably know one or two persons who are happy with their jobs, who manage their financial affairs perfectly, and who always seem to be content with whatever they purchase. This is more than just good fortune. It comes from a source of inner wisdom. The exercises in this book will guide you toward this source of inner wisdom.

ACKNOWLEDGMENTS

I wish to acknowledge with deep gratitude three persons whose contributions helped make this book possible.

My teacher, Dr. Freda Morris, founder of the Hypnosis Clearing House, Inc., in Oakland, California. It is she who kindled within me the "fire of desire" to become a professional hypnotherapist.

My colleague Jesse G. Kray in Richmond California, who reviewed painstakingly the technical aspects of this work. His suggestions were of the greatest benefit to me.

My friend Ronald J. Stockman in San Francisco, who helped me patiently in editing and organizing the manuscript.

FINANCIAL WELL-BEING THROUGH SELF-HYPNOSIS

chapter one

LIVING IN A STATE OF FINANCIAL DIS-EASE

WHAT IS FINANCIAL WELL-BEING?

I've often been asked whether a seminar on financial well-being through self-hypnosis could teach a person to go into a trance and come up with a list of winning stocks. Unfortunately, self-hypnosis has its limitations in predicting the future. Even if you could pick stocks through self-hypnosis and become immensely wealthy, this would not guarantee financial well-being. Howard Hughes, despite all his billions, certainly was not in a state of well-being.

I define financial well-being as a state that enables us:

1. To derive our income in an enjoyable and meaningful way.
2. To make enough money to meet our true needs.
3. To manage and use all our resources to further our enjoyment of life.

How to realize these three goals is what this book is all about.

For most of us, achieving even one of these goals is an unattainable dream. This is because most of us don't *allow* ourselves to know what we really want to do, don't perceive the financial opportunities available to us, and don't understand our true needs.

CONFLICTING MESSAGES

In every area touching on our financial well-being we constantly receive conflicting messages. Examples:

> In inflationary times you should buy today what you'll need tomorrow, because prices are bound to go up.
>
> BUT
>
> In inflationary times, when interest rates are high, you should use your funds to invest wisely. By locking in these high interest rates, you make sure that when inflation abates, your return on your investments will be extremely high.

Both statements are perfectly correct, but they cancel each other out.

> If you want to climb the corporate ladder fast, you must be willing to work very hard, give it your all, fight for what you want, and when necessary be ruthless and intimidating.
>
> BUT
>
> A person who follows such a course is prone to heart attacks, high blood pressure, nervous stomach disorders, and a host of other psychosomatic ills.

Is the investment advice we receive any sounder?

> In the late 1970s investors returned to gold as the ultimate inflation hedge. Ads appeared stating that one ounce of gold bought a fine suit of clothes a century ago, and the same ounce would buy one of equal quality now. Gold, unlike paper money, never lost its value. So you take your savings and exchange them for gold coins.
>
> BUT
>
> You discover that Smart Money has "discounted" gold. It has departed to money market funds. With such high interest rates, the latter is now the new inflation hedge.

Vocational advice, in the form of computer printouts, tells you everything you need to know about a specific job—except whether it will be available when you finish training for it. For instance:

> You have a vocation for teaching but decide against it because the postwar baby boom has been over for quite a while. Reluctantly you decide to become an aerospace engineer. Upon graduation you discover that visiting the planets is out and a balanced budget is in.

How about guidance in spending your money wisely?

> Surely you can trust the most conservative of our institutions—our banks. Your friendly bankers mail you an unending stream of credit cards. Presumably, they want you to use them. So you do.
>
> BUT
>
> You find yourself so deeply in debt that you have to turn your paycheck over to experts who manage the affairs of terminal debts cases. Often these experts will handle clients only if they are willing to destroy their credit cards.

WHO HAS THE ANSWERS?

When we try to follow the conflicting messages we get from the experts, we either go in circles or stand still. Mostly, our actions cancel each other out. Somehow we've gotten stuck in a dead-end job, we find ourselves outsmarted by the Smart Money, and all we have to show for our efforts is a pile of debts.

It isn't that we aren't used to conflicting messages. Politics and religions, for instance, inundate us with such messages. We deal with the former by thinking things through and making up our minds, and we deal with the latter by trusting our beliefs.

The trouble is that whatever touches on our financial well-being is readily measurable. When you buy stock, it either goes up or goes down. You either get promoted on your job or remain stuck in your old position.

When it comes to measurable things, we usually go to people in the know, like physicians, engineers, and scientists. We expect accurate answers, and we usually get them. When we don't, we become very distressed. "The doctors don't know what is wrong with me" has an ominous ring to it, because if they don't know, then who does?

So, if the answers of the "experts" in the field of financial well-being don't serve us, to whom do we turn? Perhaps we should turn inward and listen to our own counsel. The trouble is that we have been conditioned to do just the opposite.

IMPRACTICAL PRACTICALITIES

From early childhood on we have been trained not to indulge our whims. We've been trained to conform to schedules and social norms, to sacrifice spontaneity for practical considerations. Jenny can't play with her dolls before breakfast, and Bruce must do his homework before he can ride his bike. Both Jenny and Bruce must learn to save their allowances if they want to have spending money for Christmas.

So well are we trained that, as adults, we subject our most cherished hopes and aspirations to the same rule of not indulging our whims. We equate not playing with dolls before breakfast to not pursuing a career we really like and understand. As a result, we might spend our lives at meaningless drudgery.

To add insult to injury, this "practical" attitude often causes us to diminish our financial welfare. You may spend your entire working life earning less than your full potential because of a "practical" decision. You want to become, say, a registered nurse. Somehow you get the "practical" message that, in your case, and in these days, it would be more advisable to become a practical nurse—two rungs below an RN. Years later you'll repeat endlessly the same refrain: "I should have become an RN, but now it's too late."

MINDS IN COLLISION

In the following chapters we discuss our conscious and subconscious minds more fully. For the moment, let's just state that our conscious mind deals with the logical parts of our thinking. It is this aspect that makes us thinking human beings. Thus, for example, we alone, among all living beings, can adapt ourselves to living underwater, on the ground, in the air, and in outer space. Obviously, using our conscious mind must be an essential step in reaching any decision. By not using it properly—by being illogical—we will surely contribute to our financial dis-ease.

Our subconscious mind governs our feelings and emotions. In it reside joy and sorrow, love and hate, and all our dreams and hopes. Unfortunately, our dreams and hopes are often antagonistic to our logical, conscious mind. When we ignore or overrule our subconscious mind, we equally contribute to our financial dis-ease.

When our conscious and subconscious minds are working harmoniously, we can achieve anything we really want. When they collide, as is so often the case, we pay a frightening toll—living in a constant state of dis-ease.

BEING CONTENT WITH OUR DECISIONS

If we know how to obtain answers from within ourselves, are we guaranteed better results in our vocational and financial undertakings? Not necessarily. However, we are guaranteed that we will be able to live more comfortably and harmoniously with our decisions. This in itself will contribute to a feeling of well-being.

Let's look at two *hypothetical* examples.

Suppose you have come into some money and want to make an old dream come true by buying a home for yourself. You think about the joys of growing organic vegetables in your garden, owning two huge dogs, and all the other privileges of being your own landlord. You soon discover that now, for some obscure reason you don't understand fully, is not the time to buy a house. People in the know buy Treasury bills or invest in money market funds and sit tight, collecting enormously high interest. In five or ten years, you are told, when the inevitable crash in the housing market touches bottom, you will convert your Treasury bills into cash and pounce on a bargain.

So here you are, living in a cramped apartment, dreading the next rent raise, and keeping a goldfish for a pet. For another set of obscure reasons, which you also don't understand (nor does anybody else!), the real estate crash has been postponed to the beginning of next century. Yes, you've earned a lot of interest over the years. But with all this money you still feel frustrated and unfulfilled.

In the meantime, had you listened to your subconscious, you might have enjoyed your dream house and reaped the financial benefits that automatically go with it: reduced income taxes, no rent increases, and a forced savings program through mortgage payments. If and when the real estate bust arrives, you still have your home. Puttering in your garden and playing with your dogs, you can look forward patiently to a new real estate boom.

Accountants will reassure you that in the long run you will do better financially by not buying a house right now. Life, however, is made up of a series of short runs. Sitting pretty thirty years hence doesn't make up for a daily feeling of frustration. And are you sure you'll be around thirty years hence?

Now let's look at the reverse side of the illustration.

You've come into some money. You feel that it is time for you to do the things you have always wanted to do, mainly traveling and studying. If you invest your money wisely—say in high-yield, short-term bonds—you'll have enough income to do all the things you want. If you don't spend all your income but reinvest part of it, you may even preserve your capital.

So you consult the money experts. They feel that you must buy a house. These days, they say, when you invest in anything, the interest doesn't even match inflation and taxes. Only real estate keeps going up and up. Thirty years hence, when you retire, your mortgage will have been paid off and you will be living free and clear, collecting your pensions. *Then* you can travel and study all you like. So you give up on your trip around the world, your yoga courses in India, and your harp lessons at home. You buy not only a house for yourself, but following sound advice, a duplex you can rent out to help pay off the mortgage. How much more practical can you get?

You've traded freedom for the duties of a landlord: the inevitable repair hassles, the screening of tenants, the putting in a new kitchen floor during your vacation.

Ten years down the road you finally realize that you've had it. You just want to sell the house and take your trip around the world. You'll have to settle for a smaller appreciation of your property, but you're willing to do that. Just to be free and start traveling! You discover that real estate values have plummeted. There are rumors that the law will change and mortgage payments won't be deductible from income tax. In anticipation of a total crash, homeowners have started getting rid of their homes, and the market is saturated.

The experts' record for predicting future events is very poor. But we can discover what we want and need now. (Knowing what we need now doesn't preclude planning for the future. We may feel *now* that we need to be secure in our retirement years, for example, and embark upon a substantial savings program.) To do this we have to find a way to tap into our subconscious to get in touch with our true needs and wants.

This is where self-hypnosis comes in. It enables us to get uncensored messages from our subconscious. These messages are then evaluated by our conscious mind. Whatever our decisions will be, they will come from our entire being.

chapter two

SELF-HYPNOSIS: A TOOL FOR DISCOVERY AND CHANGE

IGNORING OUR SUBCONSCIOUS MIND

Social living requires that we regulate, overrule, or ignore many of our physical desires and emotional expressions.

When I feed my two cats in the morning, the large male, after finishing his food, checks the second cat's dish. The smaller female is a slower eater, and when the male comes to her dish, she yields and moves away. He then finishes whatever is left over. Of the three of us, only I am upset by this routine. I want the male to learn to be fair and eat only his own portion. But his mother didn't teach him the abstract concept of fairness, nor that one could suppress the urge for food and be a nobler cat for it.

Were he—the cat—a young boy, he would get an earful about being a little gentleman, being fair to his younger sister, and, most important, that one shouldn't always satisfy one's cravings.

Human beings learn to regulate their excretory impulses, govern their sexual drives, and master their emotions by hiding pain, anger, or hurt when appropriate. We become adept at ignoring, or at least temporarily controlling, many physical functions. Our efforts are not always successful. We manage to stifle quite a few yawns out of courtesy, but sometimes one slips by.

For the sake of simplicity let us refer to areas not under the control of our conscious mind as areas governed by our subconscious. By the time we are mature adults, most of us have learned to respond to messages from our subconscious in a selective manner. Some we obey instantly; others we ignore or repress. The most dramatic instance is a soldier charging into withering enemy fire, knowing that he is going to his death. Any other animal would do just the opposite—it would flee.

Since we're so proficient at ignoring messages from our subconscious, we can also find it relatively easy to do so in matters relating to our financial well-being. Say you've just started a very well-paying job. The only drawback is that it involves constant exposure to loud noise. You start to get headaches, feel irritable, and experience loss of appetite. The subconscious is sending out warning signals. You choose to ignore them, because you feel you'll never get another such well-paying job. You may even rationalize the situation by saying to yourself that all jobs give people headaches.

THE SUBCONSCIOUS TAKES REVENGE

What happens when we continually ignore our subconscious? Let's use a hypothetical example.

Ruth is in her early thirties. She dropped out of college years ago and became a secretary. An intelligent and pleasant young lady, she advanced rapidly and, after a few years, became an executive secretary. The pay is excellent, and she has the use of a car; her assignments take her to international vacation spots. Gradually she starts feeling dissatisfied with her job. She has a vague feeling that she would be more fulfilled back in school, studying music. As a secretary she has reached the top. As a musician she feels she'll have a more meaningful career.

She dismisses these feelings. Even if she wanted to give up her position she couldn't do it, because she wouldn't have the funds to support herself and pay for her tuition. Besides, she has proved herself as a secretary. As a musician she's an unknown quantity, even to herself.

The subconscious mind can take two different tacks to "get even." It can start tripping her. The subconscious is very good at it. We blush when we least want to. Our tongues slip to reveal exactly what we want to keep secret. Under the stress of an exam our minds go blank.... Ruth might develop a mysterious allergy, conveniently around the tips of her fingers, making typing impossible. Or she might develop a sudden aversion to her boss, whom she used to like, which may, eventually, cause her to resign or be fired.

The second tack is more common and more insidious. Like water seeking its own level, the subconscious can compensate for its frustrations by encouraging all sorts of escape behavior: overindulgence in food and drink, doing drugs, excessive gambling, or similar self-destructive conduct. It would hit Ruth in an area where she is most vulnerable. If she has had a slight weight problem, she'll start gaining pounds. If she has always been somewhat extravagant in her shopping, she'll spend her money so foolishly that she'll incur heavy debts.

Because Ruth's problems stem from her subconscious mind, the only solution is to get in touch with it and somehow work things out between it and her conscious mind.

GETTING IN TOUCH WITH THE SUBCONSCIOUS

There are a number of ways of getting in touch with the subconscious. The psychoanalytic approach, among others, attempts to accomplish this. However, such an approach is costly and time-consuming, and for this and other reasons many people are reluctant to avail themselves of it.

Issues bearing one's financial well-being are not always the province of the therapist. They call for a harmonious approach based on the subconscious mind's allowing and supporting a given action while the conscious mind, embodying one's knowledge and experience, analyzes and approves it. A therapist might not be the ideal person to consult because he or she might not have the background to understand the problem at hand. The "correct" answer is available from within, if one knows how to get to it.

This is in no way denying the usefulness of any form of therapy when necessary. However, financial well-being decisions can be reached on a routine basis through self-hypnosis. It is simple to learn, fast, readily available, and free.

APPLICATIONS OF SELF-HYPNOSIS

Many books have been written attempting to explain what hypnosis is and how it works. Yet the subject is still shrouded in mystery. In spite of anything you might have heard, basically only three mental phenomena occur in a hypnotic state:

1. The critical faculty is bypassed; that is, the conscious mind is, to a certain extent, neutralized.
2. We are in an altered state of consciousness; that is, we are in the subconscious mode.
3. We are more receptive to suggestions than under ordinary circumstances.

There are also some accompanying physical responses, which will not be discussed here.

Returning to Ruth and her problems; self-hypnosis would be an ideal tool for exploring her subconscious feelings about studying music and, if appropriate, making use of suggestions to facilitate her return to college. Through self-hypnosis Ruth can first of all discover whether her desire to go back to college is a serious matter or a passing fancy. By way of illustration: Every now and then the weather where you live might get to you—too hot, too cold, too rainy ... At such times you might wish you were somewhere else, where the climate would be exactly the opposite. You can readily discover through self-hypnosis whether you really want to relocate or whether you're just having a pleasant fantasy to cheer yourself up. (You will learn these self-hypnosis techniques later on.)

Once Ruth discovers that the desire to give up her job and take up music in college is serious and deeply important, she needs to assess her skills as a musician. Will she be successful in a music career? It may seem strange, but her intuitive insight, which is facilitated in a state of hypnosis, might be just as valid as the various opinions of her instructors. Try to recall a time when *your* intuition had told you that you would be able to perform a certain task well, long before you acquired the necessary skills. From childhood on we learn to ignore our intuition and to use rational thinking instead. But our intuition is often more accurate than our logic. (How often, after making a mistake, have you said to yourself, "I had a feeling that this wouldn't work"?)

Ruth still has to work out a plan for financing her education. We'll come back to her in the next chapter. In the meantime, by using self-hypnosis, she may have an additional benefit: It is possible that by reestablishing a harmonious relationship between her conscious and subconscious minds—her intellect and her spirit—her allergy or her drinking or her gambling might diminish or even disappear.

THE POWER OF SUGGESTIONS

In our conscious mode of thinking we use directions. We learn a dance, for instance, by following directions: Take one step back and two steps forward. We communicate with our subconscious mind in a much subtler and more complicated manner. Let's try an experiment. Read these instructions carefully. Then, when you're through, conduct the following experiment.

Stand up straight and close your eyes. Take three deep breaths. Now raise your arms in front of you to shoulder level. Imagine vividly that in your left hand you're holding a pail of water; a very, very heavy pail. It's so heavy that you can barely carry it. Now imagine that a huge helium balloon is tied to the wrist of your right hand. The balloon is pulling your wrist up and up. Your hand and arm are getting lighter and lighter. The left arm is heavy; the right arm is so light. Keep imagining this scene for a minute or so. Now open your eyes and notice the position of your arms.

I have conducted this experiment with numerous groups of people, and the results are always more or less the same. A few members of the audience move their arms rather markedly. Their left arm will be pointing almost straight down and the right arm will be at chin level. Most members of the audience experience some movement. A few don't move their arms at all.

Notice the following:

1. Some people accept suggestions more wholeheartedly than others. A few don't accept them at all. (The reasons for this phenomenon are of great interest but are not pertinent to this work. However, be aware that your subconscious may reject your own suggestions, just as if the hypnotist were another person.) In short, unlike directions, the results are unpredictable.
2. The suggestions address themselves to the imagination, not to rational thinking.
3. The suggestions themselves do not mention movement. The movement occurs as a *result* of an *imagined* situation.
4. The suggestions are not based on a real situation. There are no balloons or pails.

Suggestions, once accepted, are more powerful than directions. Consider the placebo effect when drugs are tested. The group receiving the placebo often does nearly as well as the group receiving the real drug. The suggestion that a patient has received a healing substance can often create spontaneous healing. Yet the same patient would probably not respond to a physician who *directs* him to get well by next week.

The most important aspect of suggestions is that they need not be related to the present reality. It is this fact that gives them their great power. What you suggest is *not* true; it is, rather, the truth told in advance. It resembles a tree. You plant a seed (the suggestion), and a fruit-bearing tree will grow from it. Not all seeds take, and not all suggestions work. When they do work, the results are rather spectacular. The most spectacular ones are the visualized suggestions, which we'll discuss in the next chapter.

chapter three

THE VISUALIZED SUGGESTION

WHAT WE VISUALIZE WE ACHIEVE

Maxwell Maltz, in his classic book *Psycho-Cybernetics,* states that all human beings have within themselves a "built-in guidance system or goal-striving device"[1] that enables them to achieve their aims in life. Visualization enhances this process by bringing about faster results in a more abundant form. "Our lives are limited by what we see as possible. In visualization, we expand what we have by expanding what we want."[2]

Visualization techniques work regardless of whether we comprehend the reasons for it—which are, in any case, speculative. I would like to refer the reader to a book called *Seeing with the Mind's Eye,* which discusses all aspects of this subject.[3] The book also has exercises for people who find visualizing difficult. (Visualizing is more than just "seeing." This point will be taken up in Chapter 9.)

[1]Maxwell Maltz, M.D., *Psycho-Cybernetics* (North Hollywood, CA: Wilshire Book Company, 1974), p. 14.

[2]Adelaide Bry with Marjorie Bair, *Visualizatigon: Directing Movies of Your Mind* (New York: Barnes & Noble Books, 1979), p. 40.

[3]Mike Samuels, M.D., and Nancy Samuels, *Seeing with the Mind's Eye: The History, Techniques, and Uses of Visualization* (New York: Random House, 1975).

Guided visualizations are different from daydreaming or fantasizing. They are exercises designed to bring about specific results. Certain mental conditions make these exercises more effective: concentration, relaxation, and being in touch with the subconscious mind. Such conditions can be brought about through self-hypnosis.

THE BENEFITS OF VISUALIZING

Earlier I referred to visualization as a suggestion. Let me elaborate on this. Suggestions made in a state of hypnosis to bring about certain changes are posthypnotic; that is, they take effect *after* the hypnotee comes out of hypnosis. A visualization is an embodiment of a posthypnotic suggestion. If you see yourself twenty-five pounds lighter six months from now, the suggestions that you eat less and exercise more are *implicit* in the visualization. How else will you lose the twenty-five pounds? Like any other suggestion, your subconscious mind may accept or reject the visualization.

For our purposes, visualization has another, equally important use. We can visualize a variety of *hypothetical* situations and gauge our subconscious reactions to them, without having to make any commitments. By way of illustration: Assume you've received a job offer in a field that is very enjoyable to you. It's really a very special position that may never come your way again. But the salary is much too low. Your conscious mind rejects it out of hand. Your subconscious mind, in visualization, tells you that you will be extremely happy at this job. The visualization has given you a *sense* of the situation without a commitment one way or the other. Now you can weigh the pros and cons without overriding your feelings.

OPENING NEW OPTIONS

A lot of mysterious aspects are associated with visualization techniques. Consider, for example, that Marquette University has been offering seminars in the uses of imagery in the healing arts. One of the topics is imagery in the treatment of cancer, discussed by Dr. Carl Simonton. On a less esoteric level, visualizations achieve great results because they open new options to help us attain our goals.

Let's return to Ruth's case, which we discussed in the preceding chapter. Assume that her reason for dropping out of college was that she had had a series of disagreements with her parents and she no longer wanted to be supported by them. The repeated visualization of going back to college will reopen the option of being supported by her parents. This option has always been open to her—her parents actually told her so—but as far as *she* was concerned the matter was closed. Now that she has decided to resume her studies, the visualization created the means to make this come true.

Since human beings are goal-oriented, their mental computers usually come up with elegantly simple and efficient solutions. In a soap opera she would have done something far more dramatic. In real life she found the obvious solution by giving herself permission to change her attitude toward her parents. Her conscious mind probably rationalized her behavior as being in her *parents'* best interests.

Visualizations, when strong enough, will override other considerations and create an obsession. This can easily lead to the belief that the end justifies the means. The conscious mind must do the logical and moral evaluation of the means created by the visualization. The need for cooperation between the conscious and the unconscious leads us to a related subject.

LEFT AND RIGHT BRAIN HEMISPHERES

Our left brain hemisphere governs our analytical and logical thinking, that is, our sequential way of thinking. The right hemisphere governs our holistic and intuitive perceptions.

Thus, when we make use of an automated teller, we use left-hemisphere-type thinking. The computer communicates only sequentially. Our holistic understanding of money matters won't help us deal with the machine. Unless we follow every step precisely as instructed, we won't be able to withdraw or deposit funds. On the other hand, when we "get" a joke, it is not words we understand but the totality of the situation. Our right hemisphere perceives the funniness. Our verbal ability resides in the left hemisphere. This hemisphere is the larger and, in most instances, the dominant one.

Usually we experience no difficulties in understanding our left hemisphere's way of thinking, and to a certain extent we control it. (For instance, we can switch from one language to another; we can debate, logically, both sides of an issue.) We often have a hard time understanding why our right hemisphere reacts the way it does. We find it difficult, if not impossible, to control phenomena like emotional swings or feelings of apprehension. Self-hypnosis allows us to have more access to what is going on in our right brain hemisphere.[4] Visualization makes it possible for us to influence *future* perceptions. (For instance, you can visualize yourself enjoying the dreaded yearly party your boss gives at his home. The visualization can change your attitude toward this event, so you will enjoy it.)

Influencing future attitudes through visualization is an important point in Maltz's *Psycho-Cybernetics*. His contention is that the mind does not distinguish between an actual experience and an imagined one. Visualizations therefore can train the mind to perceive a future experience in a different light than it perceives the experience at the present moment. Visualizations serve the same purpose for the mind that physical training plays in sports. Present training influences future performance.

THE HARMONIOUS MIND

One hears a lot of nonsense these days about "right-brain thinking" being superior to "left-brain thinking." We are better equipped for survival by having two fundamentally different hemispheres that in tandem help us cope with the business of living. If we have to carry a heavy and bulky object, we use both hands for the task. One might do the trick, but it would make the task awkward. Throughout this book I suggest that you utilize your subconscious and conscious minds and your left- and right-brain modes of thinking to achieve *harmonious* results.

[4]This is a fascinating and complicated subject. If you wish to pursue it further, I suggest you read Richard M. Restak, M.D., *The Brain: The Last Frontier* (New York: Warner Books, 1980).

It is said that Edison and Einstein had sudden insights that gave rise to their inventions and theories. Such insights are right-hemisphere phenomena. But these insights were not based on factual ignorance. Similarly, if you want to invest in a new venture, an intuitive inspiration based on factual knowledge will be of great advantage. Investment inspirations based on ignorance usually turn out to be financial disasters.

Our left hemisphere solves problems in a vertical manner, very much the way we deal with an algebra problem. Our right hemisphere works laterally; it forms new concepts and thought patterns, not necessarily derived from the old ones. This book emphasizes an innovative approach to financial well-being situations. Such approaches are more easily visualized than verbalized. Again, to evaluate the feasibility of such visualizations, the analytical left hemisphere has to be put to work.

There seems to be a great deal of similarity between the left brain hemisphere and the conscious mind and between the right brain hemisphere and the subconscious (unconscious) mind. This has been suggested by Dr. David Galin of San Francisco's Langley Porter Neuropsychiatric Institute.[5] Basically, consciousness is an old philosophical concept. Freud's ideas about the unconscious relate to this concept. The completely different modes of thinking of the left and right brain hemispheres are new discoveries. We might be talking about similar concepts but using different terminology.

This is all very speculative. What is important for our purposes is that both the subconscious (unconscious) mind and the right brain hemisphere understand and respond more readily to the language of imagery than to verbal commands.

BELIEVING, WANTING, AND DESERVING

Since I have written extensively on how visualizations materialize, you may ask why all the terrible things we constantly visualize don't come true. (Don't you sometimes visualize all the things that might go wrong with your car on the freeway?)

[5]Ibid., p. 199.

There are three ingredients necessary to make a visualization materialize: wanting it, believing it will happen, and feeling that you deserve it. Of the three, the last one is the most difficult to understand.

Whether you deserve to be the president of a company, do well in the stock market, or own a luxury car is a determination that comes from deep within yourself at a subconscious level. It has absolutely nothing to do with the facts of the matter. The most obvious illustration I can give deals with people who hold political power. It is quite obvious, on a woldwide basis, that many political leaders do not deserve to hold office. People who are more deserving than these leaders will agree with this assessment; yet these people do not think that they are deserving enough. So the undeserving are in office, and the deserving ones disqualify themselves because they don't think they are equal to the task.

Bad things people visualize often do happen if they want them to happen, believe they will happen, and feel they deserve the punishment. Somehow, for good things to happen, we must feel that we deserve these things. To a large extent this is tied in with the way we perceive ourselves, our self-image. (If you want to pursue this topic further, I suggest you read Maxwell Maltz's *Magic Power of Self-Image Psychology.*[6])

[6]Maxwell Maltz, M.D., *Magic Power of Self-Image Psychology: The New Way to a Bright, Full Life* (Englewood, NJ: Prentice-Hall, 1964).

chapter four

DOING YOUR OWN THING

EVALUATING OUR OCCUPATION

When the hippies roamed the land, they were fond of saying that they wanted to do their "own thing." For a group advocating a simple way of living, this was, from a practical point of view, an inconsistency. The greatest *luxury* one can aspire to in life is doing one's own thing. In the words of playwright Christopher Morley, "There is only one success—to be able to spend your life in your own way."

If you think this is an overstatement, ask yourself whether your relatives, friends, and acquaintances are doing their own thing. How many people do you know who are even moderately happy with their occupation in life?

I suspect that society has a vested interest in people doing not their thing but society's thing. How this works out in practice is a mystery. What is certain is that society fills its vacant positions, but the arrangements rarely please the people who fill these vacancies. In the olden days, when people couldn't choose what they wanted to do when they grew up, they regarded work in a more realistic light. The book of Genesis describes it as God's curse on Adam, equal in severity to Eve's punishment, the pains of labor. The Greeks thought that productive work should be left to slaves.

Through self-hypnosis you can be one of the relatively few members of society who manage to do their own thing. For this you need to know what your thing is, to allow yourself to do it, and to find a way to actualize it. This is a very tall order, but the rewards are substantial.

In evaluating our way of making a living we face a number of problems. Because we get paid for our labors, we tend to use money as a yardstick to measure the worth of whatever it is we're doing. This is a completely unreliable criterion. It is a matter of public record that many successful actors and entertainers, on whom society has bestowed untold riches, have turned out to be deeply unhappy, even to the point of committing suicide.

Our social prejudices assign values to different modes of earning a living. In theory, therefore, physicians as a class should be more fulfilled people than, say, plumbers. This is certainly not a true generalization. It is this sort of thinking that often propels people into positions with which they can cope intellectually but for which they are unqualified emotionally. How many people can admit to themselves, let alone to others, that though they're quite intelligent, they lack ambition, are basically lazy, and disdain responsibility? With such qualities they would do very well as minor civil servants. But, due to social pressure, they find themselves in jobs requiring precisely the qualities they do not have.

The Peter Principle,[1] only half in jest, stipulates that most people are locked into the positions for which they are most unsuited. What is probably even truer is that, lacking a means to tailor our occupations to our personal needs, we spend our lives locked into a position with which we're uncomfortable. And this discomfort often stretches right into retirement, another occupation for which many people are not suited.

We can use self-hypnosis to liberate us from this fate. But before that we must free ourselves from three myths.

[1]Laurance, Peter, *The Peter Principle* (New York: Morrow, 1972).

THE THREE MYTHS

Myth 1:

"I'm too old to change careers." Grandma Moses took up painting because of physical frailty at the age of seventy-six. Her best work was done when she was one hundred years old.

Myth 2:

"The job is lousy but the pay is good." (Or, "I could stand the job if I got paid more.") I remember being interviewed for a "genteel" social worker-type position. The interviewer, a pompous man, kept postponing my queries about the salary that went with the job, intimating that with this sort of a position the psychic satisfaction far outweighed financial remuneration. Money *is* a major consideration; after all, it is what work is all about. But your pay is a compensation, not a bribe. You're selling your skill and your time, not your soul. If a job is lousy at $25,000 per annum, it is equally lousy at $50,000 per annum, even if the job includes benefits like a terrific pension, an outstanding medical-coverage plan, a car, an expense account, or whatever. A good frame brings out the beauty of a painting; it does not convert an ugly work of art into a splendid creation!

Myth 3:

"I don't enjoy what I'm doing but I'm good at it." (Or, "It's the only skill I have.") When we have invested many years and much money in perfecting a skill, we find it difficult to give it up just because we don't enjoy it.

From childhood on, I have had a flair for legal thinking. Even as a youngster I could read and understand legalese. On the other hand, I have always had negative feelings about the legal profession. Friends and relatives always told me that I ought to study law, that I was a natural for it. I spent one semester in law school and did extremely well. Fortunately, I had the good sense to get out before I got sucked into the career. I can visualize myself as a lawyer: successful, prosperous, respected, and also deeply unhappy, resentful, and cynical. If you're good in one area, chances are you're also good at something else. You must decide which of your skills you're willing to sell and which you will use only for your own purposes.

The first thing you want to discover through self-hypnosis is what you would really like to do with your life. You may discover, for instance, at the age of thirty, that you would like to become a ballerina. You studied ballet for many years and were pretty good at it, but you never thought of it in terms of a career. Well, you're obviously too old to become a professional ballet dancer. However, with your dancing experience you might make an excellent ballet teacher. When you're successful enough at it, you might even open your own school. "But," you say, "I'm making a lot of money as a secretary and I've got job security." Doing your own thing often demands the courage to take risks.

You may realize through self-hypnosis that you enjoy a certain amount of physical danger and even recklessness. You may then ask yourself whether you would be happier, say, as a deep-sea diver or a firefighter. It is in this context that money matters, pension plans, and social prestige should be considered. Between these two you might as well choose the more practical one.

SELF-HYPNOSIS AS A CAREER AID

If you feel unhappy with your present state of affairs but don't know what you want to do "when you grow up" (and you may already be pushing fifty!), the self-hypnosis exercises will help you discover your untapped resources and skills. This process may take quite a while—weeks or even months. For whatever reason, these resources have been hidden from your conscious mind for a very long time and are not readily accessible. It is worth the effort, though. Late bloomers often produce the prettiest flowers.

There is a special group of people who prove that, with ingenuity, in an economically free society, it is possible to switch careers at any age and prosper. Political refugees, unlike ordinary immigrants, often arrive in this country with no readily marketable skills. Take a man who was a lawyer in his native country. Unused to manual labor, and probably too old for it in any case, he is desperately seeking a source of income. Typically, he and his family might open a small restaurant serving their native dishes. After a while they do as well as, or even better than, they did as a lawyer's family in the old country.

Of course, such changes are a result of calamitous circumstances. But what can be done out of despair can also be accomplished out of simple desire for change. If you are unhappy with your present occupation or career, self-hypnosis can bring out the same ingenuity in you that dire necessity brings out in some political refugees.

USING VISUALIZATIONS

Visualizing in a state of self-hypnosis will also help you when you are looking for a new job or embarking on a new undertaking. As we've already discussed, the mere intense visualization of an event makes the event more likely to happen.

As an added benefit you'll also do better in your job interviews. For a while I worked as a résumé writer. It has always amazed me how few people prepare themselves for interviews. They're often not even ready to deal with a problem they're painfully aware of (for example, having been fired from their last job) and find themselves improvising during the interview. By visualizing the interview you not only prepare for it, you're actually changing your attitude toward it, from mild anxiety and apprehension to a state of positive anticipation.

You may be happy with your career in general but so distressed by your working conditions that you feel you want to move into something entirely different. Gifted and dedicated teachers, for instance, often feel this way when they work in blackboard jungles, for boards of education that are solely interested in accurate statistical data. They know that there are more rewarding teaching positions available in private schools, institutions in remote areas, and elsewhere. These positions don't pay as well, or they might be far away from the big cities. In the calm of self-hypnosis you may realize that you can do with less pay and that getting out of the Big City might actually be a blessing.

When we are stressed, we don't think creatively. This is why so many people perish in a panic situation, overlooking an obvious way out. Self-hypnosis allows for the calmness necessary to find the unlocked exit. For instance, you might like everything about your present place of work; your supervisor, however, makes things so miserable for you that you feel you must give up all your benefits and start somewhere else. In a more tranquil state you might realize that you can ask for a transfer to another department. In order to do this, you'll have to take a course in shorthand. Reflecting on it in self-hypnosis, you'll realize that circumstances are moving you into a better spot. Shorthand is a skill worth acquiring.

On occasions we must work at something we dislike intensely so we can guarantee the income we need to prepare for another career (like the music student, who gives piano lessons to reluctant children). This might become so repugnant to us that we are willing to give up our major goal. Chapter 8 deals with this problem and points out a different approach through self-hypnosis.

For the sake of financial well-being you'll have to face changes in your life and, very likely, even have to make sacrifices and take risks. When we face the prospect of doing something we intensely dislike (and that can range from being a dentist to working as a dishwasher), day in and day out, for well over 70,000 hours, making sacrifices and taking chances are not all that bad! The few who are happy with their work often develop daring and ingenious tactics to obtain their goals.

THE TEACHING LETTER CARRIER

I'll close this chapter with one such example. When I was the director of adult education at a community center in San Francisco, a man dressed in a letter carrier's uniform filled out an application as a sculpture instructor. It turned out that he had been a college instructor in the fine arts department for many years. The head of the department told me that the applicant had been a dedicated teacher but refused to conform to faculty rules and policies.

The letter carrier told me that he had finally decided to do the art teaching his own way. He found a job that assured him a decent salary and security. He liked outdoor work. As a letter carrier he was a loner; he worried more about getting bitten by dogs than he did about his supervisors.

He turned out to be a very unconventional instructor but well liked by most of his students. The center didn't have policies, quotas, paperwork. As long as his classes had enough students, all he had to do was to sign in. As a free-lance instructor he ran his own show. He could move from one position to another without jeopardizing his livelihood, his medical coverage, or his retirement plan. To be able to teach art his own way, he was willing to give up the prestige of being a college instructor. He gained intellectual freedom and *enjoyed* both jobs.

As you do the self-hypnosis exercises, you'll notice that you start thinking along unconventional lines. Doing your own thing is by definition an unconventional undertaking.

chapter five

OWNING, NOT BEING OWNED

WHAT WOULD YOU BUY IF YOU HAD A MILLION DOLLARS?

Imagine the following scenario.

Jim is a young, single schoolteacher with a modest income. A distant relative dies and, to Jim's surprise, leaves him an estate of one million dollars. As soon as Jim receives the funds he rushes out and buys the home computer he has always wanted. It's the best available on the market. The more Jim uses the computer, the better he likes it.

Jim owns a relatively new car, a basic American model with few options. Now that he's rich, friends urge him to buy a car befitting his station in life. Jim toys with this idea, maybe just to impress his dates. Eventually, out of boredom during his summer vacation, he buys a sports car, an Italian job that can accelerate from zero to seventy miles per hour in the blink of an eye, loaded with electronic gadgets, and equally at home on the race track and on the freeways.

Now Jim spends a lot of time at the car dealership. For every part the car needs (and it needs a lot of parts), urgent messages are sent to Rome. Under normal circumstances the parts arrive within two weeks. When there are strikes in Italy, which is often the case, it takes as long as it takes. Much of the time Jim drives the old clunker the dealership reluctantly loans him or rents a car for which he has to pay dearly. Nostalgically he remembers the good old days when he brought his car to his trusted repair shop in the morning and picked it up after school.

Our possessions tend to become our masters and own us. We need to choose carefully whom we want as our masters. The self-hypnosis exercises will help you distinguish between the things you really need and want and between the things you *think* you need or want.

Jim knew positively that he wanted a computer. He had known this long before he had the money to buy one. He was made aware by friends, and by his new circumstances, that he wanted a sports car. The trouble is that however disillusioned Jim becomes with his Italian car, he'll never revert to the basic car he used to drive. He has grown attached to luxuries he never knew he would like. They've become necessities. While the computer has enriched his life, and he's already planning to buy an even better one, all his future gadget-loaded cars might serve him *less* than the car he had in the old days.

Relative to this, the popular BBC program *Upstairs, Downstairs* imparted an important lesson: If you own a mansion and entertain royalty, you must resign yourself to spending a goodly amount of time dealing with the romantic involvements of the scullery maid and the footman. The property we own always comes in a package deal: what it will do for us and what we will have to do for it.

SLAVES TO PLASTIC CARDS

Since Jim's example belongs to fairy tales, we need to consider a second point: that most of the time the funds for our beloved gadgets and white elephants are borrowed. The Bible says, "The borrower is slave to the lender."[1] Most people don't feel that they're the slaves of the banks that finance their homes, cars, and gadgets. More subtly, they become slaves to their working conditions. The

[1]Proverbs 22:7.

more you own, the less flexible you are to make changes at work. If husband and wife work, both are locked into their jobs. It is, for instance, anticipated overtime pay that enabled them to buy their second car. It is also the overtime that creates their marital discords.

By and large, societies tend to encourage some form of indebtedness. It keeps citizens from doing their own thing and forces them into the economic mold. The landowners who advance seed money to their tenant farmers, to be paid back at harvest time, create generations of semislaves bound to the land. Working to pay off the dishwasher, dryer, or what have you distorts your relationship with your employer. You don't just need *a* job. You need *the* job you have *now,* you need the overtime that comes with the job, and you must have your annual raise.

I've included a number of suggestions and visualizations in the self-hypnosis section for readers who want to deal with their debts. In some cases, getting out of debt is the first step toward becoming economically free. For some people this means destroying their credit cards; for others, it means an austere period of paying off rather than acquiring. By ridding yourself of oppressive debts, you gain more flexibility in almost every area of your life.

THE MYSTERIES OF CREDIT

Credit is a subject full of ironies. It is offered lovingly when you least need it and is withdrawn capriciously when you need it most. We are told that we ought to establish credit even if we don't want it, but we are also taught that borrowing is dangerous and borrowing too much is reckless. (Governments are obviously excluded from the folk wisdom!)

The fact is that borrowing when you manipulate the situation makes good business sense and borrowing when the lender manipulates the situation has inherent dangers in it. For example, if you use your credit cards to charge purchases and pay for them months later, when your statements are due you've leveraged your money. If you remit the minimum monthly payment and pay a horrendous interest rate, you've borrowed money on very unfavorable terms.

THE MASTER PLAN

Usually it's the availability of credit that allows one to indulge in impulse buying, out of love for the object, frustration, boredom, or whatever. There's nothing wrong with impulse buying as long as it doesn't enslave you further through debt. One way of going about shopping is to make an annual master plan. If you want to buy a dishwasher, surely it would make more sense to buy it when it is on sale, so schedule it for January rather than for December. When making your annual master plan, you may discover that you can't afford a dishwasher and a stereo and all the new clothing you need during the next twelve months.

In a state of self-hypnosis you can visualize having the desired objects and *not* having them. Between the stereo and the dishwasher, which do you want more? The visualizatiaon might make you aware that your life is lacking because you don't listen to good music. On the other hand, a dishwasher won't add very much to your happiness. You may even decide to establish a special "dishwasher fund" and save enough so you can buy one in two years.

A master plan has another advantage. People often feel guilty because they don't know whether they can afford the particular item they're about to buy. Often they don't even know whether they really need it. By planning on a conscious and subconscious level, you know that you need what you're about to buy and that you can afford it.

The rich often shop wisely without a master plan. It is they who buy Christmas cards on December 26 when they are marked down fifty percent; it is they who buy bathing suits in January and expensive sweaters in July, when these items are on sale. The master plan gives you the same advantage. If you need a pair of new skis, you can *plan* to buy them at the end of the season.

A good master plan will allow for impulse buying by earmarking a certain amount of money for this purpose. If you're poor, it might be just enough for an expensive blouse you see on sale; if you're well-off, it might allow for a painting sold at an auction. Children, too, can be taught to develop a master plan. They too can learn to visualize what would suit their needs and desires and make their own annual choices. Obviously, it makes no sense to ask children to express their desires and then overrule them as impractical.

LACK OF FLEXIBILITY

When I was the principal of a private school, I had the opportunity to observe two groups of parents: the poorer ones, whose children were granted partial scholarships, and the more affluent ones, who could barely afford the full tuition for their children. The poorer ones somehow managed to handle the annual increments on the partial scholarships; the more affluent ones had to apply for partial scholarships to cope with the increments. The scholarship committee frowned upon these requests because, given the parental income and life style, they should have been able to pay full tuition.

The richer parents simply lacked financial flexibility. They were locked into a situation in which every expense was rigidly fixed and pointing upwards: the home mortgage, the finance charges for the two cars, the children's tuition and orthodontics. Even their entertainment expenses couldn't be cut without serious social consequences.

Unlike the truly wealthy, theirs was an artificially high standard, based on borrowed funds. They lacked flexibility to accommodate themselves to new economic realities. The price they paid was the terror of having their wealth bubble burst and losing some or all of their unpaid-for acquisitions.

TAKING CHARGE OF YOUR LIFE STYLE

Certain items must be purchased in conjunction with our jobs. On the most basic level these include apparel to fulfill the employer's dress code (for example, uniforms for nurses). Things get more subtle and more expensive as positions become more lucrative. Real estate salespersons have to drive cars respectable enough to chauffeur their clients around. An attorney whose firm specializes in tax shelters must give his clients the impression that he himself is wealthy enough to use such shelters. The Mercedes he drives may give this impression, though the only shelter he seeks is from the creditors yapping at his heels.

If you're required to join a golf club when you would rather spend your money on skiing, to drive a glamorous car when you would rather own a power boat, it's time to take stock of whether you are in charge of your own life. The greatest danger is that after a while you think that your job *affords* you the Mercedes, whereas it is your job that *forces* you to drive one.

On such rarified levels things get very convoluted. The availability of expense accounts, tax write-offs, and company perks can force us into a style of living we might not *really* enjoy. A trip for yourself and your spouse to Acapulco is great, provided you really like tropical beaches. Having to reciprocate invitations by giving receptions where alcohol flows like water becomes an expensive burden, especially if you don't enjoy this type of event.

Financial well-being means acquiring the items, including luxuries, that will enrich your and your family's lives. Financial disease means spending your funds to acquire goods and do things dictated by your position at work or by social obligations. Because it is so difficult to distinguish between the former and the latter, self-hypnosis is a useful tool for this purpose. The self-hypnosis exercises for this chapter have been devised for this purpose.

chapter six

MAKING ALL THE MONEY YOU NEED

GOING AFTER THE THINGS YOU WANT

The authors of *Money Madness* make the point that the "primary reason that more people do not make more money is that, despite their longing, money is not worth what it would take to get it."[1]

Financial well-being does not mean having more money. It means having enough money for what you need and want. In the preceding chapter I discussed how self-hypnosis can help us determine what we truly need and want. In this chapter let's deal with how, through self-hypnosis, we can obtain the financial means for these purposes.

Being rich is an abstract concept, always in need of a new definition. If you have $10,000 in savings you might think that $100,000 would start you on the road to riches; with $100,000 you would realize that it is hardly enough these days to give you even a modicum of security; at $1 million you would understand that you've just reached the basement of wealth. And so it goes. Rather than becoming rich, which is an endless pursuit, it is easier to strive after the things we need and want, which is a goal-oriented endeavor.

[1]Herb Goldberg and Robert T. Lewis, *Money Madness: The Psychology of Saving, Spending, Loving, and Hating Money* (New York: The American Library, 1979), p. 192.

For example, a client of mine, with whom I worked on finding a new career, asked me to suggest to him, in a state of hypnosis, that he make "a little more money." (He worked as a supervisor in a plant and moonlighted as a part-time salesman.) I asked him why he needed the money. His first answer was that it "always helps to have extra money." After some reflection he said, "What I really would like to do, if I had the money, is buy a house." In a state of hypnosis I had him visualize the house he wanted to buy, see himself and his family living in it, feeling the enjoyment of coming home from work to his own house. Actually, the down payment on a house would take more than just "a little more money." But a house is a very tangible goal that can be visualized clearly and, for most people, a goal they really desire and need rather than a fantasy item like a yacht. This is the type of visualization that translates readily into the real thing.

ECONOMIC FREEDOM

It is common for people to feel locked into their economic positions. A teacher's aide might expect just to get by, whereas a lawyer would take it for granted to be quite well-off. It is the expectation that often gives rise to the reality. This sense of being locked in carries over to earning more money. People who work in a factory think of overtime; if they work as bookkeepers they think of keeping the books of two or three small businesses on the side. All of it doesn't amount to substantial sums of money. Worse yet, it becomes even more of a daily grind.

Practically all schemes for earning a substantial extra income are of an entrepreneurial nature, which means they're viable only in societies that allow and favor this kind of activity. These schemes are usually quite ingenious because they draw on people's skills and interests rather than on their financial resources.

For example, a bank teller I know specializes in raising exotic goldfish, which he imports from Japan and Hong Kong. He runs his business out of a one-bedroom apartment that is full of aquariums. He caters to hobbyists who order his fish because they know them to be healthy. He started his business as a hobby, and it caught on rather spectacularly.

Often his customers will call him with fish health problems, and he prescribes over the telephone. He's expert enough to disagree about fish health maintenance with published books on the subject. He could not leave his teller's job and work for outfits selling goldfish. They would never hire him because he has had no education in this field. This suits him fine. He does things his own way, and after a day's work with the public, and under the thumb of supervisors, he prefers to minister to his "beautiful fishies," as he calls them, who tend to be on the quiet side.

TWO ILLUSTRATIONS

When I was a school principal I discovered that the toughest and least thankful duty I had to perform was the supervision of the janitorial staff. A school runs well only if the janitors perform their duties properly. Supervising three part-time janitors seemed to absorb more time and energy than running the entire school.

One day a former janitor came to see me with a business proposition. He had just started his own janitorial service—a small operation, mostly with part-time help, looking after small businesses. What he had to offer was his know-how and his willingness to cope with constant absenteeism and complaints. I gladly turned over the school's business to him and thus solved one of my major problems.

He did well. Had he chosen to work longer hours as a janitor, he would never have been able to approach his income as a businessman. (He would also not have faced the risks inherent in owning a business.) He freed himself from being locked into a fixed income for the rest of his life, doing it with limited financial resources and educational background.

For a number of years I worked in the Latino section of San Francisco. Many women there were employed as seamstresses or in similar positions, drawing the minimum wage for very hard work. Many of these women were quite skilled at sewing. One lady translated this sought-after skill into something far better than factory work. She discovered that laundries, which did not have sewing facilities on their premises for minor alterations and mending needed by customers, had a hard time finding somebody who would take over this task. She associated herself with a few such laundries, making a good living from her home. Her investment consisted of a sewing machine, which she had always had, and her skill as a seamstress.

I am certain that the janitor and the seamstress didn't use self-hypnosis to tap their hidden resources. I am almost certain that on some level they visualized a future more abundant than what they could have expected under ordinary circumstances. In any case, they were among the enterprising few who were willing and able to improve their financial well-being through their own initiative.

Self-hypnosis provides the proper tool to anybody willing to use this skill. First, it points the way you can break out of your present condition and attain what you want. Second, it encourages and guides you along the way, so that one or two failures won't be the end of your efforts.

In societies where free enterprise is encouraged there is always a way to generate money in a manner unrelated to "one's station in life." Selling is a good example, because it requires little, if any, formal training. Selling cosmetics, vitamins, or household products in conjunction with parties or social gatherings can be quite lucrative, if done properly. True, it isn't the income a lawyer realizes out of a million-dollar malpractice case, but the salesperson doesn't have the same overhead or investment in time and energy. (People who market these selling schemes usually introduce novices to salespersons whose incomes exceed those of lawyers!)

VISUALIZING A WAY OF MAKING EXTRA MONEY

Let's use a hypothetical illustration of how one can achieve extra income for a desired goal. Imagine a fifty-year-old man, whom I'll call Bruce, who works as a supervising shipping clerk for a mail-order house. It is his twenty-fifth year on the job, and he can opt for early retirement after thirty years. He and his wife decided a long time ago that upon his retirement they would buy a small farm, ten acres or so, and use the income from it to supplement his pension. They've saved for many years toward this goal. Now, five years away from retirement, they're some $25,000 short of their goal.

Bruce realizes that he will have to find something not related to his job for extra income. These days there is no overtime available where he works. He takes stock of his skills and talents. He is a good driver and knows his city well. So he has the qualifications for moonlighting as a cab driver, and his neighbor, who owns a taxi, will let him drive it. Now let's suppose that Bruce uses visualization techniques. He realizes immediately that being a cabbie is not what he is all about, so he dismisses the notion.

As he visualizes, he becomes aware of a whole set of skills he has. He is the family's and the church's handyman. Hardly a week goes by when he isn't helping somebody to put in a floor, install an electric outlet, fix a leak in the roof, or build a wall. Everybody is appreciative, and at Christmas time he gets a lot of nice gifts. He hears again and again that handymen are difficult to find and are often incompetent or dishonest.

As he visualizes, Bruce becomes aware that he can earn a lot of money if he starts charging for his work as a handyman. He wonders who his customers would be. Surely he couldn't charge his family or the church. Seeing himself working at the church points him to a source for finding his first customers. He will advertise in the church bulletin. Members who know him and have seen the quality of his work will want to use his services. Once he has a few satisfied customers, word of mouth will do the rest.

Now you say that one doesn't need visualization or self-hypnosis for such a straightforward, rational sequence. But remember that Bruce's first impulse was to become a taxi driver. This would have been a simple undertaking. Bruce would have had a pretty accurate idea of how much money he could make per hour of driving and therefore know ahead of time how to arrange his schedule.

The handyman plan was much more complicated and unpredictable. However, financial well-being means not only making the extra buck but also being comfortable doing it. For Bruce, being a handyman is a meaningful undertaking, and he'll enjoy his relationship with his customers.

Of course, Bruce might have miscalculated. He might not make as much money as he needs for the farm. Financial well-being doesn't mean financial certainty. Such certainty doesn't really exist; it is goal-oriented toward a meaningful future, but it is also concerned with a worthwhile here and now.

FOCUSING ON THE GOAL THROUGH SELF-HYPNOSIS

For some ten years I held a part-time position as a college instructor. When I gave up the job, I had had my share of frustrations and irritations with the institution. I decided I would never teach there again. About a year later I went to hypnosis school. While I studied, I became aware that teaching self-hypnosis would be a natural for me, having been an instructor most of my life. I started visualizing myself, with great emotional intensity, giving classes on this subject. As my visualization gathered a momentum of its own, I saw myself receiving invitations to speak before audiences and starting my private practice through referrals from my students. (Incidentally, all this came true within a startlingly short period.)

About two months before I graduated I started looking for a teaching job, only to find that I had no chance whatsoever of finding one. New teachers in any subject have a difficult time, and hypnotists in general are considered to be on the scary side. Can you imagine me saying, "I would like to teach self-hypnosis in your college. By the way, I'll be graduating next month"?

During one visualization session I had a sudden insight. In the entire universe there was only one teaching institution that might consider me: the one I had worked for. They at least knew that I could teach and might give me a chance for old time's sake. But what about my vows never again to be connected with that institution? It was the intense visualization of teaching self-hypnosis that gently nudged me to visit one of my former supervisors who was in charge of such classes. He was fascinated with the subject, though somewhat skeptical. It was a friendly chat rather than a job interview.

He gave me two classes, and I started teaching one week after my graduation. From that position it was much easier for me to find other teaching jobs. As an added benefit, I didn't even have to bother with the paperwork that comes with a new teaching assignment, because all my credentials and personal data were on file.

Of course, I could have done it without visualization in a state of self-hypnosis. It was the logical thing to do. Chances are, though, that it would not have taken place without the motivation of visualization. My logic would not have overcome my great initial distaste for reemployment at my old college.

FINANCIAL WELL-BEING AND INNER HARMONY

The hypothetical illustration of Bruce is not very spectacular. Rather, it's typical of how ordinary people can make, in a meaningful way, the money they need to achieve a particular goal.

Writing in a different era, Napoleon Hill, in *Think and Grow Rich*,[2] gave much more dramatic examples of people who visualized their way to enormous riches. Hill himself considered Andrew Carnegie his mentor. Reading this and his other books is certainly a profitable undertaking.

Hill was obsessed by the notion that by becoming wealthy people automatically solve all their other problems. (As a matter of fact, he considered poverty *the* problem.) According to Hill, poverty equals misery and riches bring bliss. It's easier for me to accept the former than the latter.

To me, financial well-being means having what you want and need rather than being able to acquire anything you see and fancy. Bruce and his wife visualized ten acres of their own. They could have visualized twenty and would have attained that goal just as well (though it would have meant hiring people to work their land, which seems contrary to their retirement dream).

The difference between these two points of view can be seen when visiting Hearst's Castle in San Simeon, California. It contains

[2]Napoleon Hill, *Think and Grow Rich* (New York: Fawcett, 1979).

William Randolph Hearst's incredibly expensive and rare collection of art objects from all over the world, housed in splendid surroundings. The collection is arranged in a mismatched, irrelevant, and meaningless manner. Originally the castle housed as much as Hearst could stuff into it; the rest was stored in warehouses! It is a monument testifying to the fact that with money one can buy anything. What it sadly lacks is a sense of harmony, wholeness, and purpose. If, through visualization techniques, you can achieve harmony and purpose in your life, you will come closer to financial well-being than by becoming immensely wealthy, with no particular purpose behind your riches.

If you ardently desire funds for a specific purpose, you can bring about this outcome. The purpose itself may be practical (like a home) or urgent (like an operation). Or it may be just a pleasant venture. An African safari can be visualized and materialized in the same manner.

Then why isn't everybody prosperous and content? When you work as a hypnotherapist, you soon realize that the people who give up smoking or lose unwanted pounds are those who are really, earnestly, wholeheartedly committed to these goals. The rest also want it, but in a different way: They want to lose their desire for smoking or overeating; then, naturally, they won't need to indulge a desire that no longer exists. They are unwilling to experience the desire and also experience *not* satisfying it. Similarly, most people desire more money without wanting to experience the work and pressure involved in obtaining it. To break out of any status quo situation you need additional energy to overcome the inertia inherent in the status quo. Self-hypnosis supplies the spark that fires the mechanism of making money.

chapter seven

AT PEACE WITH YOUR INVESTMENTS

THE WITHERING STOCK

You are a young, restless, eager investor ready to parlay your very modest savings into a small fortune. Your broker calls you with good tidings. His firm is underwriting a new issue of a small company that is going public.

The company's product is an agricultural implement needed all over the world. The company makes most of its money abroad, so it doesn't depend only on one market.

Brokers are under great pressure to push new issues underwritten by their firms. You, as an investor, have the advantage of not paying a sales commission on the trade when you buy a new issue. Also, it is your chance to get in on the ground floor of a future IBM or IT&T.

So you buy a hundred shares at $20. Your broker assures you that the issue is underpriced. He estimates, conservatively, that the stock will go to $40 within the next two years: a tidy profit of $2,000, with minimal tax consequences. Of course, the new issue doesn't pay dividends. The company plows back its profits into expansion. Capital growth is the name of the game!

Time passes and your stock, far from growing, is shrinking alarmingly. You call your broker, and he has a handy explanation:

The U.S. dollar is too strong vis-à-vis other currencies, and customers abroad can't afford American-made products. Given the present economic climate, the strength of the dollar could not have been foreseen.

Fifty-one weeks later you get another call from your broker. He tells you that the stock now trades for 7⅜. He suggests that we (it is always "we") sell before the year is up, so that we can take advantage of short-term capital loss. After commission your loss will amount to some $1,300. Your broker knows of a new issue, coming to market next month, at $8. The company behind it manufactures an item needed and wanted by all mothers who care for their babies...

Who is to blame? Nobody!

ARE YOU A GOOD LOSER?

This situation is known as an "investment mistake." If you want to make spectacular profits, you must expect some reversals as well!

Sad to say, all investments carry risks. So when you refer to a "safe" investment, anytime, anywhere, always put *relatively* ahead of *safe*. When you open an account with a broker, this message doesn't sink in. The form asks you whether you're investing for income or capital appreciation and the like but not how you feel about the inevitable losses. Even more significantly, how do you feel about *potential* losses?

In the stock market one experiences real losses and paper losses. If you buy a hundred shares at $10 and they decline to $7 you have suffered a paper loss of $300. By the next day the loss might total $400. This is an unrealized loss. You may eventually sell the shares for 14 and realize a gain of $400. Will you worry yourself sick while you suffer these paper losses?

You need to ask yourself a number of questions: How much am I willing to risk? How do I feel about the possibility of losing money? How do I feel about losing my entire investment?

The exercises relating to this chapter will help you get in touch with your subconscious feelings toward the preceding questions. If you discover that you don't like losing money, does it mean that you can't invest? Does it mean that you must stay away from the stock market?

Not at all.

YOUR OWN INVESTMENT PLAN

Just as much as you need to examine your subconscious feelings about risk taking, you need to increase your conscious knowledge about whatever investment you choose. Then you can present an investment plan to your broker. It will indeed be "we" when you and your broker work in tandem.

When you study investment strategies, you will discover that there are all sorts of mixtures that can be used for your stock portfolio. As *one* example, you can invest in utility stocks. These tend to be relatively safe as far as steady, substantial income is concerned. They usually increase their dividends on a regular basis, and, when inflation is not running amok, they may actually appreciate.

Why doesn't your stockbroker tell you about such opportunities? One reason is that conservative stocks are meant to be kept for many years, and your broker is interested in fast-moving papers. In your case he is also on firm ethical grounds. Conventional wisdom has it that young people are supposed to invest aggressively (and lose aggressively?) and utilities are for widows and orphans.

WHY NOT DEFER TO THE EXPERTS?

There are lawyers to handle our legal problems and physicians to take care of our physical ailments. Why not turn over our investments to the experts in this field? To answer this question, we must examine two aspects of this issue: first, the nature of economic predictions, and second, the nature and function of the experts.

The Eternal Economic Mess

Barbara Tuchman, in *A Distant Mirror,*[1] suggests that the fourteenth century was in many respects akin to the twentieth. In France in 1351, for instance, the currency suffered eighteen devaluations.

> Under Jean II, manipulations were so frequent and erratic that they upset all values and succeeded in damaging and infuriating everyone except the manipulators themselves and those who could profit by holding back their gold. Abbot Gilles li Muisis of Tournai found the mysteries of the coinage even more obscure than the plague and was inspired to a famous verse:
>
> *Money and currency are very strange things.*
> *They keep on going up and down and no one knows why;*
> *If you want to win, you lose, however hard you try.*[2]

As far as predicting the future of economic developments is concerned, little has changed since the fourteenth century. Professor Ezra Solomon of Stanford University (and a former member of President Nixon's Council of Economic Advisors) said about economic forecasting, "It's the only thing that makes astrology look respectable."[3]

Rational forecasting, even in times of peace and prosperity, is impossible because governments mismanage the economies of their countries. Because the economies of most countries are intertwined, one country's mismanagement can create havoc with other countries' economies. Some governments mess up the economy through the application of ideological or political policies; others do so all too often out of sheer ineptness—so much so that even when good things happen to the economy, governments often manage to turn them into disasters. A recent outstanding example is Mexico. No sooner did the Mexican government discover that the country was floating on a sea of oil ("the Saudi Arabia of the Americas") than it went on a borrowing binge. This brought about runaway inflation, rampant unemployment, and further

[1]Barbara W. Tuchman, *A Distant Mirror: The Calamitous 14th Century* (New York: Alfred A. Knopf, 1978; ©Barbara W. Tuchman, 1978.)
[2]Ibid., p. 136.
[3]*San Francisco Chronicle,* October 18, 1982, p. 49.

destabilization of the once sound peso. The relatively prosperous Mexican economy declined rapidly, and the country became internationally bankrupt in the summer of 1982.

Enter the economists, whose task it is to predict and shape the economy. Governments seek their advice but usually don't follow it to the bitter end. Since different schools of economics prescribe different cures for the same ailment, the politicians feel free to change course abruptly. This allows the economists to blame the politicians for the mess and thus absolve themselves. What economists usually excel at is explaining, in retrospect, why things haven't worked out.

In this connection, one would assume that banks have on their staffs brilliant economists to safeguard their investments. The Mexican fiasco endangered the integrity of the American banking system, since a number of major banks were involved heavily in loans on which Mexico defaulted. In an article titled "Bank Responsibility for Mexico's Woes" in *The Wall Street Journal,*[4] Lawrence Rout accuses the American banks of greed and carelessness in lending money to a bad credit risk. If banks' economists cannot make valid economic predictions to save their institutions from disaster, how can a private individual hope for some sensible guidance from these quarters?

In summary predicting what the economy will do in the future is almost a futile task. If you live long enough, you can assume that the economy will go through cycles of boom and bust. If you want to be cynical about it, you can blame much of the bad times on politicians and economists and ascribe the good times to sheer luck, your personal good fortune, and a lot of intuitive insight.

Specific Investment Advice

The success of predicting the future of a given investment is also far from spectacular.

In January 1980, gold rose to an all-time high of $875 per ounce. A lot of people bought it at that price because it was

[4]*The Wall Street Journal,* October 22, 1982, p. 24.

predicted to rise right up to $2,000 per ounce within a very short period. Doomsday writers made fortunes selling books exhorting their readers to invest in gold and silver or face the prospect of becoming paupers.

From its high, gold declined to $300 per ounce in less than thirty months. Everyone assumes that international tensions cause the price of gold to go up. Well, everybody is wrong. The crisis in Poland and wars in the Falkland Islands and Lebanon actually saw a decline in the price of gold.

For diversification and personal gratification, the same doomsday writers recommended investing in "collectibles"—art, stamps, coins, and other items. "Rare coins have slumped between 40 percent and 80 percent from 1980 to the summer of 1982, and almost lost 50 percent of their value."[5] Ah, yes. What happened to the doomsday writers? They are quite well, thank you!

They decided to push a different investment. Many financial advisers suggested that their clients look at bonds. James Sinclair, a onetime goldbug, said, "The next big play there is not gold, but Treasury bills and bonds."[6] Financial advisers always do well for themselves. It is their followers who take the losses!

As to the future of gold, in the summer of 1982 there were predictions that it would go up to $4,000 in a few years[7] and, conversely, that it would fall below $300. If you want to invest in gold, *you* must make up your own mind!

The Experts' Compensation

With the exception of a certain kind of independent investment adviser, most of the "experts" in the investment field have more in common with travel agents than with doctors or lawyers. Travel agents give lots of advice. They make their commission, though, by selling trips. Similarly, stockbrokers do not make their commission by giving investment tips but by buying or selling stock for their clients. The more often, the better for them.

Financial institutions make money only when you invest with them. Your bank manager can suggest various investment plans for

[5] *The Wall Street Journal*, July 12, 1982, p. 36.
[6] *Time*, May 24, 1982, p. 64.
[7] *The Aden Analysis*, November 3, 1982 (Metairie, LA: Adam Smith Publishing), p. 3.

your $10,000. What he won't suggest is that you take your money to a savings and loan a block away to earn an additional ¼ percent.

A PERSONAL EXPERIENCE

The clouds darkening the Mexican economic skies had gathered a few years before Mexico defaulted on its international loans. This was fairly obvious to any informed reader who followed the Mexican economy. The only ones who were ignorant of this situation were the people who count—international bankers! They seemed to be unaware, for instance, that in 1981 alone short-term loans totaling some $20 billion had been advanced to Mexico.[8]

In the summer of 1981, Merrill Lynch, Bache Halsey Stuart, and Salomon Brothers gathered a syndicate of international underwriters with august names like Aramco International, Daiwa Europe, Deutsche Bank, and Swiss Bank Corporation and decided to underwrite a closed-end mutual fund. Listed on the New York Stock Exchange, this fund would invest exclusively in Mexican stocks. As Mexico prospered, so would the investors of the Mexico Fund. It went public in June 1981 at the offering price of $12 per share.

When I saw the news bulletins about this fund in May 1981, I asked myself whether the timing wasn't all wrong for investing in the Mexican economy. I called my broker for a prospectus and told him how I felt about it. He said that he didn't know much about the fund but "take a good look at the underwriters!"

Well, I took a good look. Could I know more than the legions of seasoned economists working for these investment firms? Obviously not! So I overruled my gut feeling and suspended my intellectual analysis, in deference to the Wise Ones. I limited myself to a hundred shares. Within months the price of the shares reflected the realities of the Mexican economy: I sold at $4 per share and the price kept going down.

Do you get the feeling that the above is sour grapes? Of course it is sour, very sour grapes! Not because I lost money but because of how it happened.

[8]Susan Lee, "New Rules To Throw Light on Bank Loans," *The Wall Street Journal*, November 5, 1982, p. 30.

A closed-end mutual fund of this type is what Wall Street is supposed to be all about. It's an investment vehicle, not a trader's speculative ploy. It went sour because the experts neglected to do their homework. But the way the system is set up, the experts don't need to be successful. The underwriters of the fund made their commissions; the managers of the fund will continue to draw their salaries; the special corporation serving as the fund adviser will go on dispensing advice. As long as there is action—buying or selling—everybody makes money. Everybody except the investor. Moral: Don't ever assume that the experts are particularly concerned with making money for *you*. This is *your* responsibility.

TAKE CHARGE OF YOUR INVESTMENTS

You are not in good hands by blindly following the advice of the person who handles your funds. Consider him a technician. The investment *policy* is your responsibility. This policy evolves through your dedicated reading of the financial section of the newspaper, general investment literature, and specific investment information.

When you invest in the stock market or in real estate or even just deposit your funds in the bank, you are taking a risk. The higher the risk, the more substantial the potential return. By being savvy and market-wise you increase your probability of doing well with your investments. By being the policymaker it will be easier for you to live with the consequences.

The self-hypnosis exercise that goes with this chapter will, among other things, motivate you to learn all you can about investments in areas of most interest to you.

YOUR INVESTMENT PORTFOLIO SHOULD REFLECT YOUR PERSONALITY

You may wonder why I have suggested learning about investments in areas of most interest to you. After all, the purpose of investing is to make money, not serve as a source of amusement. This is undoubtedly true for many investors. For them it might be enough to understand thoroughly their investment field. However, many people are turned off by investments because they find just reading about the subject a monumental bore.

You can invest—and make money—in such diverse fields as art prints and pork bellies. If you are artistically inclined, reading about prints might actually be enjoyable to you. If you make a mistake and have to take a loss, at least it will be a lot easier to bear than having taken the wrong position in pork bellies.

Your medium of investment should represent your personality, temperament, philosophy, and interests. If you're a conservative person, you might favor bonds. You can make, and lose, just as much money with bonds as with "go-go" stocks. However, bonds exude conservatism. If you are interested in ecology, you may want to invest in solar-energy issues. If you believe in the imminent collapse of the economy, gold investments might be urgent.

There is a great feeling of satisfaction when you receive a shareowners' report that you enjoy reading and can evaluate intelligently. It is much easier to motivate yourself to do the necessary homework if you are interested in the subject.

MUTUAL FUNDS

If you are just beginning your investment program, have limited funds at your disposal, and are not sure where and how to invest, mutual funds are the answer.

The funds offer numerous advantages. First, you can invest, on a regular basis, relatively small amounts. (Regular small investments are safer than a single large investment.) Second, these funds are so diversified that it is highly unlikely that your small investment will be wiped out (or, for that matter, that your small investment will bring you spectacular results). Third, you can learn the "secrets" of the trade by watching the "pros." (One such secret is that half the time the pros are wrong! This is an important lesson. You learn early to be skeptical and cautious.) Fourth, you will be inundated with investment literature. As time passes, you will assimilate more and more information, including the tie-in between investments and tax strategies.

The fifth advantage is the most important. There are mutual funds for every imaginable investment goal: growth, capital preservation, income, tax shelters, among many others. There are funds specializing in foreign investments, environmental issues, precious metals, bonds, options, and utilities. There are even funds that invest in stocks that are out of favor and in companies that are bankrupt!

As eloquent testimony to the fact that even pros don't outperform the market in the long run, there are funds that mirror the market performance. If you invest in one, you are reasonably certain that your $1,000 will do just as well, or as poorly, as the market in general.

With a modest sum of money you can choose a number of funds and invest in them for a while. It is an inexpensive and *relatively* safe way of obtaining an education. After a while you will know which is suited for you. See Chapter 11 for sources of information about mutual funds.

CAN YOU AFFORD THE EMOTIONAL RISK?

Investors tend to be a nervous bunch of people driven by greed and checked by fear. The following quotes are typical of what one reads daily in the financial press (the italics are mine). "Gold prices plummeted $10 per ounce on traders' *nervousness* over the course of American interest rates."[9] "Most interest rates fell slightly yesterday, but many investors remain *nervous* about economic and money supply figures to be released today and tomorrow."[10]

How nervous can you get before it affects your emotional well-being?

Since *all* investments involve an element of risk, the obvious question you must ask yourself is whether you can afford to lose

[9]*The Wall Street Journal*, July 15, 1982, p. 29.
[10]Ibid., p. 38.

part or all of your principal. The not-so-obvious question is whether you can afford *emotionally* the threat of the actual loss of your investment.

Imagine the following scenario. You invest a substantial part of your savings in raw land, because there is an excellent chance that the city will build a new airport in that area. It seems that once the decision to build the airport has been made, you will quadruple your investment—within a short period and with minimal tax consequences. All of a sudden the bad news pours in. The driving force behind the airport idea, the mayor, is defeated in an election; the federal government issues a preliminary report stating that the area is unsuitable for an airport; another city plans to build an airport that will serve the entire region.

In the meantime, each year, you must pay the tax on your land. Under some circumstances you may have to take out insurance to protect yourself against some hobo's tripping over a log on your property and suing you. The years pass. The land is now worth one-third the price you paid for it. If you sell, at least you'll get out of the tax payments and will be able to invest the proceeds. However, there is the persistent rumor that an industrial complex will be built right where your land is. Should you wait just another year or so?

Before investing, you might want to ask yourself whether you can afford the emotional stress of having half your savings immobilized for years on end; whether you can cope emotionally with the possibility, however slim, that you might lose almost the entire investment; and, going back to the illustration, whether such a "to sell or not to sell" decision will disturb your peace of mind and affect your health and happiness. Lastly, would you be able to live with the knowledge that the whole deal has been a monumental blunder on your part?

Doing the self-hypnosis exercises, you will discover the degree of risk you can take in stride. Then, when a hot deal comes up, you'll know whether you can afford emotionally to take the plunge. Financial well-being means that you avoid situations that will be too stressful for you, even at the price of losing out on a potential deal of a lifetime.

USING YOUR INTUITION

Investors who do well consistently are not merely lucky gamblers. They usually have a great deal of expertise in their particular area of endeavor and develop a feel, an intuitive understanding. This often manifests itself in their sense of timing, which is essential for successful investing. If nothing is predictable in investments, how can one develop a feel for it? I don't know. But investors who prosper in good times and under adverse conditions often make their moves contrary to the predictions and common knowledge.

Obviously they use a rational, analytical approach. But they often benefit from an intuitive, holistic understanding. As we have already discussed, intuitive insights are greatly enhanced by using self-hypnosis or similar techniques. The exercises for this chapter will help you in developing an intuitive approach to your investment decisions, as an adjunct to rational analysis.

TAX AVOIDANCE

One cannot invest successfully without using an intelligent tax strategy. So huge is the tax bite that when you think of investment income you must immediately consider the tax consequences.

In the Oriental martial arts you are taught how to use your opponent's weight to his disadvantage. You can learn how to use the ponderous weight of the tax code to your advantage. Tax avoidance, not evasion, is the name of the game.

The rich play this game with great relish. Tax shelters see to it that the wealthy constantly suffer grievous losses. So horrendous are these losses that they sometimes escape taxes altogether. It is *because* of these disasters that they stay wealthy and grow even richer.

Ordinary folks dismiss such tax avoidance as the prerogative of the rich. Actually, the least complicated and most legitimate and common shelter is one's home. The heavier the indebtedness, the more protective the shelter.

Do you know that certain utility companies regularly classify part or all of their dividends as a "return of capital"? This means that instead of paying annual tax on the dividends you receive, you pay it as capital gains tax when you sell the stock. This tax is much lower than the annual tax.

Many people hold on to their utility stocks through their lifetime. Eventually their estate pays the tax on the accumulated dividends.

This is a perfectly legitimate tax shelter, due to an accounting quirk. While nobody knows, from year to year, the exact status of the stock, a broker can often tell you ahead of time which utility is likely to declare such returns of capital. You can avail yourself of such a shelter. To do so, you must know that such shelters exist.

TOO BORING A SUBJECT?

The trouble is that the people who complain most about the tax system are the ones who refuse to learn about avoidance. They claim either that they don't understand it or that it is too boring a subject to bother with. These are often the very same people who know all about the esoteric subject of nutrition. Learning that large amounts of zinc may cause a copper deficiency doesn't seem to be more thrilling than understanding income averaging. The former and the latter are facts one learns when one needs to know them to improve one's health or wealth.

It is absolutely essential to understand the components of the tax system that can help you reduce your tax burden. It is absolutely essential that you learn about new components that you may use in the future to reduce your tax burden even further. The more assets you have, the more you need to know about the tax system.

BECOMING KNOWLEDGEABLE

In tax matters you can get good advice from the professionals: CPAs, tax lawyers, and others. The trouble is that they charge rather handsomely for their advice. You also need to have enough knowledge so that you may ask them pertinent questions. The tax return is the result of your tax strategy; it is the wrong place to formulate one.

All you really need to do is to familiarize yourself with areas that concern you. If you invest in real estate, you don't need to know about bond amortization. If you don't have medical deductions, you need not study the subject. (You should, however, be able to research such deductions. See the reading list in Chapter 11 on this subject.)

The self-hypnosis exercises for this chapter will motivate you to become more conversant with tax matters. Understanding the tax system is a skill you can pick up, not a talent you were born with.

chapter eight

COPING WITH THE RITES OF PASSAGE

SWALLOWING GOLDFISH

Webster's definition of *hazing* is "to play abusive and humiliating tricks by way of initiating." The point of hazing is that it is pointless. It is merely the price the initiate has to pay to become initiated. It is exacted capriciously by members of a group who, in their turn, had to undergo the same humiliating procedure. On campus it might consist of swallowing a goldfish, eating a live frog, or hopping around a square like a deranged rabbit.

It seems that societies have always practiced various forms of hazing. In order to upgrade their status, members must undergo, willy-nilly, some ordeal (such as circumcision of boys—sometimes even girls—to become young adults). Anthropologists call these ordeals *rites of passage*.

There is little, if any, choosing whether we want to undergo these ordeals. They are mandated by a group we *must* join. These ordeals are often camouflaged by being called "customs," "rules," "traditions," or whatever and are alleged to spring from the collective wisdom and experience. Chinese girls as young as five were subjected to extreme pain and eventual crippling when footbinding was in vogue. In the literature of the time the beauty of females with tiny feet was extolled—especially the gracious, alluring, seductive bearing of these women. When this particular barbarism ended officially, at the beginning of this century, the poor footbound women were regarded as ugly prerevolutionary relics.[1]

By virtue of our education and training we tend to assume that behind the seeming foolishness of an ordeal hides some ancient wisdom. Being part of society, we want to assume that society knows what it is doing, even if we don't understand its actions. In any case, who are we to decide which rule serves a purpose and which is there only for general harassment?

The fact that we are unwilling or unable to recognize hazing for what it is creates a great deal of mischief. It is one thing to ask a potential initiate to swallow a goldfish as a challenge. Given a choice, he can make up his mind whether his revulsion and discomfort are worth the benefits he will derive from becoming a member of the Alpha Beta Gamma fraternity. It is quite another thing to ask him to swallow a goldfish, leaving him with the impression that it is a rational test administered for his own good or the welfare of the fraternity. The implication is that if he can't swallow the goldfish he is in some manner a diminished human being—certainly not as good a human being as those who have managed to swallow their goldfish.

From a challenge to conquer, the goldfish becomes an obstacle to struggle with. It symbolizes all a person's past failures and mistakes and discourages him from dealing effectively with the task at hand. Should he fail, it enforces a feeling of worthlessness.

How does self-hypnosis tie into this?

FOCUSING ON THE REWARD

There are an endless number of artificial barriers we must cross if we want to achieve financial well-being. We can deal with these barriers with greater ease if we regard them as mere challenges rather than rational tests of our worthiness to upgrade our status. Coping with challenges is future-oriented. We focus on the other

[1]Howard S. Levy, *Chinese Footbinding* (New York: W. Rawls, 1966).

side of the barrier. Properly motivated by the reward, you can hypnotize yourself to succeed in the initiation ritual. It needn't make sense. One climbs to the top of the mountain just "because it is there." It is difficult to cope with a barrier when your approach to it is past-oriented, that is, if you look at it in the light of your past failures. You climb it while dragging heavy chains. You bring with you your many failures at school, your three divorces, your losing battles to stay slim, your nicotine addiction, and the knowledge that it took you three times to pass a simple driver's test.

With this kind of attitude, you might need extensive therapy rather than self-hypnosis. Therapy would probably have a more lasting effect on your life and might be of great benefit. However, you may not have the time, the money, or the inclination to undergo therapy. And, usually, the challenge needs to be faced in the near future and not years hence.

HAZING THE JOB HUNTER

To illustrate how self-hypnosis can help in coping with hazing experiences, I'm going to use examples from job-hunting or career-changing situations. First, because looking for a job is an experience most of us have to face a number of times in our lives. Second, because during periods of unemployment the experience can be utterly demoralizing and dehumanizing. Third, because job hunters encounter, as a matter of course, the senseless hazing I've referred to. It is often quite obvious in this area that the rules, regulations, customs, and traditions do not originate in some deep collective wisdom but rather from prejudice, bigotry, superstition, and plain ignorance.

Consider these "minor" matters as illustrations: Until recently, males couldn't be switchboard operators and females couldn't be police officers. Yet when legislation or court rulings forced this nonsense to change, the switchboards kept on functioning and the police forces didn't disintegrate. Speaking of the police, when rigid height standards for officers were changed to accommodate short minority recruits, the force went on functioning normally.

Job-Hunting Ordeals

The first thing a job hunter needs is a résumé. The employer uses this document to screen out applicants. The vast majority of applicants automatically exclude themselves simply by sending in their résumés. (Usually the main mistake is providing too much information.) Writing a good résumé requires a great deal of experience, skill, and Madison Avenue-type hype. Where, why, and how aerospace engineers should have acquired résumé-writing skills is a good question. Nevertheless, they will be granted job interviews only if their résumé passes muster. Every now and then, especially during periods of high unemployment, one reads articles in the financial press lamenting the deceitfulness of applicants' résumés. Theologians have always pondered the moral question of whether one has a right to steal in order to feed oneself and thus preserve one's life. I wonder whether one may be less than truthful in a résumé in order to find a job to feed one's family.

I challenge the absolute truth-in-résumés advocates to obtain a job, any decent job, by conducting the following experiment. Instead of stating that their health is excellent, write in the résumé, "I spent six months in a mental hospital twenty-five years ago." Or, "I'm an epileptic, but the condition is controlled by drugs." Or, a more common occurrence, "Between 1970 and 1975 I was not always gainfully employed. I survived by taking on odd jobs and, often, collecting welfare. I was trying to find myself."

The saddest fact about résumés is that the person who does the hiring sees only the résumés of the applicants selected for interviews. The majority of the résumés are read by personnel-department clerks whose task it is to eliminate as many applicants as possible. Somehow, the same document must appeal to the bored personnel clerk who has to wade through scores of them and to the chief engineer who is looking for very special talent.

As you wear out your soles going from one employer to the next and applying at every employment agency, you're given yet another three-page application form to fill out. You have your masterpiece—your résumé—with you, but they won't take it in lieu of the application form. So you spend your precious time over an application that probably nobody is ever going to read.

After the résumé ordeal comes the trial by clothing. Employers expect applicants not just to dress neatly but to give the impression, through their clothing, that they're so well-off that they don't really need a job in the first place. In the midst of financial ruin, with your unemployment insurance running out, you find yourself being told by a head hunter that the best investment you can make at this particular moment is a new suit for your next interview.

This is followed by the interview ordeal. Your prospective employer expects you to be young but experienced, bright but not bright enough to threaten your supervisor, innovative but conformist, and ideally fit into a federally mandated slot: black, female, Oriental, disabled, Spanish-speaking.

The one thing that you find out only after you have been hired is that in this particular position nobody has lasted more than ten months. The supervisor is impossible to work with, but ... well, he is the brother-in-law of the executive vice-president.

With these kinds of challenges in mind, I have structured the self-hypnosis exercise for this chapter in a special way. You focus on the overall goal—such as obtaining a job—but you learn to cope with more than one challenge on the road toward it.

MEANINGLESS EXAMINATIONS

Taking a test when you are looking for a job is always a worrisome experience. Skill tests try to discover whether you will be able to perform specific duties well. These are relatively easy if you're qualified for the job you're applying for. There are two other kinds of tests that cause a much deeper level of anxiety. One is the psychological inventory to discover whether you have the sterling character qualities that go with the job. These are so off the wall that even self-hypnosis won't help prepare for them.[2] The other is tests that purport to measure your aptitude for the job. This is where self-hypnosis can be of great help.

Years ago I supervised a training program, under the auspices of the Office of Economic Opportunity, to prepare economically disadvantaged candidates to work for the post office. The preparation consisted of helping them attain a high enough score on the

[2]An extremely humorous and insightful novel dealing with this subject is Ira Wallach's *The Absence of a Cello* (Boston: Little, Brown, 1960).

mail clerk and carrier examination so that they would be in the running when openings occurred.

With the exception of a language-comprehension section, the test didn't examine specific areas of knowledge. Because it explored an applicant's general aptitude, there was no way, in theory, to prepare for it. In reality, once students took a dozen sample tests, they learned quite a few tricks of the trade and especially how to work faster under pressure. Often their scores improved dramatically, from the middle 60s to the high 80s. As a result of this training, the public didn't benefit by having better postal clerks. However, the students acquired a new skill: They became more competent in taking civil service examinations. By passing the test, the applicants proved that they were willing to cope with the challenge rather than that they were the best-qualified candidates for the job.

There is a whole industry helping people to better their scores on civil service tests. (Don't you wish there were a whole industry helping people to become better civil servants?) There are books, courses, and seminars, taught by specialized instructors. So successful are these programs that some applicants routinely sit for city, state, and federal tests in numerous fields. These tests certainly measure accurately the mental agility of applicants to *cope* with them and their dedication to obtain a civil service position. That these tests don't necessarily select the most qualified civil servants doesn't unduly bother the governmental agencies that administer them. From their point of view, these tests are ideal: They provide a pool of prospective employees in a fair, competitive manner. The people who have to select the new civil servants have been selected in the same manner and, in all likelihood, were also not the most qualified for their positions...

THE MATH BARRIER

Almost invariably these examinations have a math test, which for many applicants presents a particularly difficult challenge. Our approach to math is reminiscent of what previous generations thought about Latin. It was assumed that the more Latin you knew, the more logically you could think. Reading Caesar in Latin somehow made one a lot smarter than reading Emerson in English. Similarly, there is a feeling nowadays that knowledge of math improves a person's qualification for practically anything—as if knowing that $(a + b)^2 = a^2 + 2ab + b^2$ will make you better at handling an irate citizen complaining about a mistake in his property tax.

Due to electronic calculators, most people use less arithmetic on their jobs than ever before. Naturally, they forget quite a bit through disuse. It seems that the arithmetic tests are given with these factors in mind. The following is from a book preparing applicants for a civil service examination: "If, like many intelligent people, you have been out of touch with arithmetic since grammar school days, the rules and problems here should help you get back into this type of thinking."[3] All this effort just to pass an examination! You might prefer to swallow a few goldfish.

A client of mine—I'll call him Peter—is a construction worker in his late twenties. At school he did very poorly. However, he has always had a great interest in mechanics and actually supported himself for a while through this self-taught skill. Eventually he grew tired of the seasonal nature of construction work and decided to try the fireman's examination. He is in excellent physical shape and can deal well with the various sections of the fireman's test, except the math part.

Peter knows on a conscious level that when he is called upon to extinguish a fire, $7/9 \div 5/8$ would not be something he would have to cope with. So, naturally, he resents the fact that he has to restudy the arithmetic he neglected as a youngster. On a subconscious level he feels weak and threatened. His many failures in life, beginning at school, haunt him. He seriously questions his intelligence. His fourteen-year-old nephew knows more about arithmetic than Peter. Other applicants, in his evening college class, have no problems with the math. Maybe construction work is the only thing he can do...

I asked Peter to visualize in a state of hypnosis the following scene: climbing very carefully, slowly but with confidence, over a

[3]Harry W. Koch, *Fireman's Entrance Examination* (San Francisco: Ken Books, 1968), p. i.

barrier. The barrier is called the "test barrier," and the most dangerous spots are the fragile "math ledges." Once over the barrier, he sees himself as a fireman, uniform and all, at the firehouse, on the fire truck answering an alarm, and walking home from work proud of his position. I suggested to him, in a state of hypnosis, that the skills that made one a good mechanic were the same skills that one used to master arithmetic. If he looked at it this way, he would see that arithmetic was basically an easy subject, easier than mechanics, and, as a mental exercise, even fun. This examination was a challenge to test his willpower and his determination to become a fireman. I asked him to recall moments of achievement in his life and bring the same attitude to bear on this one, isolated challenge.

Peter did well on his examination, scoring in the high 80s. He now wants to sit for other civil service exams. Somehow he now sees the challenge these tests offer and manages to divorce himself from his past scholastic failures.

Anybody can swallow a goldfish once in a lifetime. By hypnotizing yourself, you might even make the fish go down without gagging. However, if you feel you've been force-fed goldfish your entire life, you might very well choke on the last one, even though it happens to be the tiniest of all.

SCHOLASTIC ORDEALS

Much of what goes on in academia, for both students and faculty members, is a hazing routine. Persons who enjoy this kind of environment cope extremely well with this way of life and, eventually, retire as professors emeriti. It is the hapless, mediocre students who struggle to overcome the artificial barriers standing between them and their careers.

Michael was an ornamental horticulture student in a community college. Ornamental horticulture, in plain English, is gardening. By bestowing a Latin-derived title to an earthy vocational subject, it has become worthy of a college course. A whole string of prerequisites have been attached to it: public speaking, economics, chemistry, and others.

Now, one would think that a "problem-solving methods" chemistry course for gardening is a splendid idea. Gardeners do work with potent chemicals. Unfortunately, this particular chemistry course doesn't, in any way whatsoever, prepare gardeners to deal with any substance more complicated than H_2O. How do gardeners handle the various chemicals they use? Same as you and I. They read the labels.

After all, beauticians, who mix potentially dangerous dyes and pour them on our heads, don't take theoretical chemistry courses. What little chemistry they have to know in order to pass their license examinations is, by and large, relevant to their work. It is intended to help them read and understand labels. Sample questions for a review test: "Can hard water be softened?"[4] And, "Is it necessary for cosmetologists to know the pH of the products they use?"[5] Gardeners have the dubious fortune of being trained in colleges as "ornamental horticulture" students, whereas beauticians attend lowly vocational schools.

Well, this isn't quite true. Beauticians, too, have their rites of passage, but less arduous ones. These days they are "cosmetologists." With a Greek-derived title one would immediately think of anatomy. Sure enough, though their text says that they "need only be concerned with the bones of the face that are affected by massage,"[6] they have to study a whole section on the anatomy and physiology of the human body.

So what's wrong with a little general knowledge? Surely it can't hurt a cosmetologist to learn some anatomy and physiology. Let me explain what is wrong with this approach by giving an illustration. To become a manicurist in the state of California one needs to know the anatomical structure of the hand and forearm, including the Latin nomenclature. (Would *you* want to be manicured by an operator who didn't know your phalanges from your metacarpals?) In theory this makes sense since manicurists massage their customers' hands. In reality, it is far from an innocent practice. A client of mine, a lady in her fifties, had had health

[4]*Cosmetology—The Keystone Guide to Beauty Culture.* (New York, NY: Keystone Publications, 1979), p. 284.

[5]*Ibid.*, p. 285.

[6]*Ibid.*, p. 249.

problems that made it impossible for her to work in a standing position. The Department of Rehabilitation paid her way through manicuring school. Her major learning problem was memorizing the Latin names of the bones and muscles. Having been out of school for well over thirty years, a completely insignificant aspect of her future occupation became her major concern. (Obviously, one can learn how to give a good hand massage without knowing Latin anatomical terms!)

Such practices create a great deal of mischief. First, these types of prerequisites severely restrict the number of entrants into a given field of endeavor, by requiring qualifications in unrelated areas. Second, they create or expand unproductive industries that help prepare students for their examinations. Third, they make services less competitive and thus more expensive. Fourth, by having students concentrate on frills (for instance, public speaking for gardeners) they restrict the time, and sap the energy, that should be spent on mastering the vocational aspects. Fifth, they make life more complicated and difficult than it needs to be, without serving a useful purpose. That is what rites of passage are all about.

Getting back to Michael; he had a true vocation for gardening. Even as a child he puttered around gardens and plants. His scholastic aptitude was mediocre; his experiences in grade school and high school were rather dismal. He had a difficult time coping with a number of courses not related to gardening but somehow managed to pass them. The "problem-solving methods" chemistry course defeated him. After a third unsuccessful attempt at the subject, he switched to radiology because that chemistry course wasn't a prerequisite. He gave up his life's ambition. Society, who foots the bill for his education, will get an indifferent X-ray technician instead of an inspired gardener.

Self-hypnosis could have helped him in two areas. First, he would have learned to regard the chemistry course as the final and greatest challenge before becoming a gardener. It would have encouraged him to get in touch with his previous academic achievements (passing another chemistry course that was difficult for him) rather than regard this course as a culmination of all his past scholastic failures. Second, by concentrating only on the problem at hand, he might have found new ways of handling this challenge. He might have taken a tutor, seven days a week if necessary, who would have taught him enough to get a passing grade. Or he might have discovered some other ingenious way to climb over this barrier.

The self-hypnosis exercises for this chapter will help you with your particular goldfish.

chapter nine

RECORDING AND LISTENING TO THE TAPES

This chapter will help you with the mechanics of recording the self-hypnosis exercises for Chapter 2. It will also give you some suggestions on how to listen to them for maximum benefit.

LOVING YOUR OWN VOICE

People who have had little experience listening to their own voice are often unpleasantly surprised when they hear themselves on tape. I suppose they would have the same reaction if they saw their face in the mirror for the first time. After a few hours they get used to their own voice, and eventually they grow to like it. Actually, there is an advantage in listening to your own voice. The suggestions come from a source you can trust—yourself.

Don't worry about making a mistake when you're recording. If it's bad enough it can be erased. If not, don't worry about it. You're not delivering a valedictory address. Your subconscious doesn't expect you to be perfect.

Speak slowly, clearly, and evenly. Let your voice be authoritative but not overdramatic. You are your own minister or teacher or spiritual guide, and your rendition should reflect that you know what you are suggesting.

If you prefer, you can order the tape I have produced. It is a ninety-minute tape and contains all the exercises in this book.[1]

ADAPTATION

The best tapes are the ones you write for yourself. Only you know exactly your particular set of circumstances. Chapter 10 will help you in composing your own tapes. Since the text of the self-hypnosis exercises is not written with your specific situation in mind, you might have to adapt certain visualizations and suggestions to your needs. Don't be afraid to do so. There is nothing immutable about these exercises. Consult Chapter 10 to make sure that you word the suggestions properly.

COORDINATION WITH THE TEXT

Before recording the tapes, you might want to reread the corresponding chapter. Start with the chapter that is most pertinent to your situation. If you're looking for a new job, deal with this first. If the subject has no bearing on your present circumstances, you'll probably not want to record the corresponding exercise. However, you might want to read the text. It will give you some insights that may be of benefit later on.

Listen to the tape a number of times, and allow at least one day between sessions. You may also want to allow some time between recording the tape and listening to it. (A few hours will do.)

IS IT DANGEROUS?

Can listening to the tapes be dangerous? No. But please observe one caution: Do not listen to the tapes in a moving vehicle,

[1]Write to Satori Tapes, 1775 Old Country Road, #9, Belmont, CA 94002. See pp. 138–39 for information.

regardless of whether you are the driver or a passenger. In other words, the *driver* of the car must not hear the tape while driving.

WHERE AND WHEN SHOULD YOU LISTEN?

Sit in a comfortable chair. You may want to use a reclining chair. Make sure your back is straight, and don't slouch. A few people tend to fall asleep while listening to hypnotic tapes and awaken when they end. (The tapes always end with the instructions to wake up.) If you have this problem, sit in a less comfortable chair or on the floor with your back leaning against a wall. If falling asleep isn't a problem, you may even do it lying in bed.

You can listen to the tape whenever you wish except before sleeping. The text suggests to you that you wake up "full of energy," which is the wrong frame of mind for falling asleep. Initially, to convince yourself that you will, in fact, awaken at the end of the tape, you might want to practice when you don't have a pressing engagement right after working with the tape.

If you want to listen to the tapes before falling asleep, you should modify the awakening instructions given in the text. Consult Chapter 12 on how to do this.

When listening to the tapes, remove your glasses. Your eyes will be closed for a while, so decide whether you should take out your contact lenses. Always uncross your legs and put your hands on your thighs.

DEALING WITH DISTRACTIONS

Make sure you are not disturbed while listening to the tape. Unless you are sure your telephone will be handled properly, disconnect it. If you experience any other distractions (an itch on your face, a barking dog), suggest to yourself: "This [the distraction] helps take me deeper. As I'm concentrating on the distraction I go deeper and deeper." This is much more effective than trying to block out a baby screeching next door.

WHAT ELSE DO I DO WHILE LISTENING?

The tapes ask you to imagine various situations. Go along with the suggestions. Almost anyone of normal intelligence can be hypnotized; imaginative people often get more out of the experience.

The instruction "visualize" is repeated often. To get best results, use *all* your senses as well as your bodily sensations. For intance, visualizing eating an ice cream cone might involve getting in touch with the following sensations: seeing the scoops and the cone, feeling the coolness of the ice cream touching your lips, testing the various flavors as you are licking the ice cream, noticing the specific smells associated with the flavors, hearing the crunchy sound of biting into the cone, feeling the slight numbness of your tongue when the cold stuff touches it, sensing the coolness of the ice cream as it descends from your mouth to your stomach, and experiencing the pleasure and satisfaction that comes with this activity.

When you hear the suggestion to visualize or imagine a certain situation, you might want to stop the tape and allow as much time as is necessary for this activity. Stopping the recorder calls for a certain conscious physical effort. To minimize this, it would be advisable to purchase a mike with an "on" and "off" button. (Most recorders provide for such an attachment.) This button allows you to stop the tape (whether it is on "play" or "record") with a slight movement of your thumb. It is a relatively inexpensive gadget. Take your recorder with you when you buy it, to make sure the prongs fit.

You will find that the mike has another advantage. It will make the job of recording easier and also give you a better-quality tape.

If you do not wish to buy the mike, practice shutting off the recorder with your eyes closed *before* you listen to the tape. If your recorder has a pause button, use it rather than the stop key.

Since it is impossible to predict how long your visualizations will last, it's impossible to say exactly how much time you should allow for listening to each segment. Between fifteen and thirty minutes is typical.

AFTER LISTENING TO THE TAPE

When the tape is over and you are back in the here and now, allow yourself to sit still for a few minutes. Never use an alarm clock to signal that time is up, as this will have an unpleasant, jarring effect.

You may want to take notes right after the tape is over. Have writing materials ready so you need not get up. The tape will also suggest to you that ideas related to a particular subject will come to you at some later time. Most likely these ideas will be fragmented thoughts. Jot them down without trying to edit or censor them. They serve as a catalyst to start a new reaction in dealing with your problems.

We have already discussed the fact that not everybody is adept at visualizing. For this reason the classical induction techniques (one of the processes that help to put the subject into a state of hypnosis) usually involve kinesthetic elements: riding a descending elevator or escalator or walking down a staircase. I have used this type of induction, though a more esthetically pleasing version of it. However, if you want variety or prefer another type of induction, I have provided two alternate versions. Eventually you'll develop your own inductions, based on your own tastes and needs.

WHAT YOU CAN EXPECT

If you experience a deep sense of relaxation and well-being during your session, you have been hypnotized. Some people go deeper than others, and some experience strange phenomena (crying, tingling sensations, inexplicable joy). What matters is that you are in touch with your subconscious and more open to ideas that under ordinary circumstances your conscious mind would have censored.

Don't be surprised if you remember everything. This is as it should be. If you "blank out," it is best to listen to the tape once again.

chapter ten

YOUR OWN SELF-HYPNOSIS PROGRAM

PRACTICING SELF-HYPNOSIS

Self-hypnosis is a skill one learns by doing. In this respect it is similar to learning how to ride a bicycle. You ride for a while with someone running along supporting you. Then, mysteriously, you're riding all by yourself. How and when you've mastered this skill is not quite clear to you. The fact is that you can do it. With practice you will do even better.

After practicing the self-hypnosis exercises in this book, you will have a sense of how it feels to be in a hypnotic state. You will also know how to get in and out of this state. You're now ready to start your own self-hypnosis programs.

In addition to enhancing your financial well-being, self-hypnosis can be useful in every area of your life. To mention a few out of a long list: stress management, motivation, skill improvement, habit control, and coping better with pain. The reading list suggests books you can read to guide you as you explore these areas.

SELF-HYPNOSIS WITHOUT TAPES

A cassette recorder has a number of advantages. It allows for separation between the hypnotist and the hypnotee. This enables you to be in a deeper state of hypnosis using your prerecorded voice to act as your guide. When listening to the tape you will be in a state of reduced consciousness, since all conscious thinking has already been done. If your mind tends to wander in a state of hypnosis, the tape will keep it more focused.

The disadvantages of the recorder result from its inflexibility. It may not allow for enough spontaneous flashes because of its rigid structure. (One way of handling this is by using the stop button on the mike, as discussed in Chapter 9.) You can suggest to yourself: "Now stop the recorder and let your mind be open to useful and helpful, suggestions." It's a free period during which the subconscious can come up with whatever insights and flashes it has in store. After a while you can return to the tape.

The second disadvantage of the recorder is that you need a unit and a prerecorded tape when you want to practice. Self-hypnosis *without* a recorder can be practiced in the most unlikely places: while you're traveling in a plane or a bus, waiting to see your doctor, or in a secluded spot on the beach.

It serves a purpose to learn how to hypnotize yourself without a recorder. You can then make use of either method, according to your needs.

CUING

When not using a recorder, you might not want to do a lengthy induction. You can learn to "cue" yourself into an almost instant state of self-hypnosis. Prepare a tape with the usual induction and then suggest to yourself:

> You're going to discover a symbol that will put you into a state of self-hypnosis easily and effortlessly. The symbol may be an object you own, like a paperweight or a ring, a geometrical form, an animal, a river, a mountain, or whatever is meaningful to you.

> As I count from 5 to 1 you focus on something of great meaning to you, which will help you with your self-hypnosis: 5, 4, 3, 2, 1.
>
> Whenever you focus on this symbol and you count from 5 to 1, you will instantly go into a deep state of hypnosis. Try it now and notice how much deeper you go....

At the end of each session suggest to yourself that next time you will go even deeper.

Remember that you want to put some distance between the hypnotist and the hypnotee. Always speak to yourself in the second person, addressing yourself as "you." It seems somewhat strange without a recorder, but you will get used to it.

PHRASING SUGGESTIONS CORRECTLY

For suggestions to be effective they must be formulated in a certain way. Before we discuss the technical aspects for formulating suggestions, let me stress once again that the visualized suggestion is superior to a suggestion that is only verbalized.

"You will be the president of the company by next year" is not as effective as "By the end of next year you will be the president of the company. See yourself performing three duties that only the president can do."

The most important aspect of formulating suggestions is to phrase them positively rather than negatively. This can be difficult because we usually focus on what *is* rather than on what *is not*. If you have a headache and you want to get rid of it, you suggest "You don't have a headache" rather than "Your head is clear." By repeating the present condition (headache), you emphasize what is wrong; by concentrating on what is right (clear head), you concentrate on the truth, told in advance. (This is why "Your headache is gone" is also the wrong phrasing.)

WRONG: You will not eat cakes, pies, ice cream, candy, or other fattening foods, no matter how good they taste.

RIGHT: You always eat wholesome foods and watch your calorie intake. When you want to nibble, you enjoy carrot sticks.

This is important to get used to, so always be aware of this point when making suggestions.

Except for special cases, which I'll discuss in a moment, suggestions are more effective when made in the present tense, even though, grammatically, the future tense seems more appropriate.

PASSABLE: You will enjoy deep and relaxing sleep every night.
BETTER: You enjoy deep and relaxing sleep every night.

When the exact date is important, you obviously want to mention it: "As a gift of good health, you'll quit smoking on your birthday." I personally prefer "you quit smoking on your birthday," so that everything is kept in the present tense. (Making positive suggestions for quitting smoking presents a problem. The opposite of *smoking* is *not smoking*. It is almost impossible not to mention *smoking* when formulating suggestions.)

Avoid challenging yourself unnecessarily.

WRONG: By Wednesday you sleep soundly throughout the night.
RIGHT: You always sleep soundly throughout the night.

Suggestions should be specific and explain what you want and why.

WRONG: You always have lots of money, so you can do whatever you please.
RIGHT: Soon you've enough money to make a down payment on a house. You earn enough to make the mortgage payments and spend money freely. You want the house because it provides an ideal environment for your family, lets them have the garden they have always wanted, and will provide you with a darkroom. It frees you from the curse of landlords and rent increases. Visualize your family working in the garden.... See yourself working in the darkroom.

If you don't really, sincerely, wholeheartedly want something, don't suggest it to yourself in self-hypnosis. If you think that speaking French would be "nice," but you have no intention of applying yourself because you don't have the time, don't make this suggestion. The suggestion is worthless, and you're setting yourself up for failure. By experiencing failures you weaken the success mechanism within you. When there is true motivation, you can phrase the suggestion in a very emotional way and in an exaggerated fashion. For example: "You become a superb public speaker because your political insights are too important to keep to yourself. As a matter of fact, you're an orator. People in the audience often compare your delivery and style to Winston Churchill's. You have the listeners in the palm of your hand. You can *make* them cry or laugh or get angry...."

HOW MANY SUGGESTIONS PER SESSION?

There are all sorts of opinions on the number of suggestions you should make in a single session. Some writers limit it to one in order to avoid confusion. Personally, I believe that your subconscious is capable of handling more than one set of ideas at a time. My own preference is to work with a number of items, say three, in unrelated fields, and tie them together. For example:

> Before I bring you back to the here and now, let me review this session. You are successful in losing twenty-five pounds within one year. Visualize yourself standing on your bathroom scale and weighing exactly 120 pounds. To your right is a calendar. Check the date. It's November 8. Just as you are successful in this area, which has always been a challenge to you, you receive the scholarship. See yourself reading the letter from the dean. And because you're a slim, trim, pretty woman, and smart enough to receive the scholarship, you are the most popular person in the sorority. Visualize yourself now being elected president of the sorority.

Notice that the suggestions are in different areas: health, scholastic, and social achievements. Notice also the praise that accompanies the suggestions. Self-hypnosis is enhanced by praise.

REPETITION

Suggestions are very much like commercials. They must be repeated over and over again until they're accepted by the subconscious mind. In a sense most suggestions an adult uses in self-hypnosis "*de*suggest" a preexisting mode of behavior. (Smoking is suggested to a young person by example or through advertisements. Self-hypnosis suggests non-smoking as a healthier way of life but, in effect, desuggests the smoking habit.) For this reason new suggestions are often accepted only after many repetitions. You may work on one set of suggestions one month at a time and come back to them after an interval if they have not been incorporated into your life yet.

AFFIRMATIONS

Emile Coué (1857-1926), a French psychotherapist, discovered that by repeating a phrase endlessly, it can bring about positive changes in our lives. This technique is called autosuggestion or affirmation. His most famous autosuggestion was "Every day, in every way, I am getting better and better." People who followed his teachings felt great improvement in their lives.

We use this method of autosuggestion every day, without calling it "affirmation." Family and societal belief systems are transmitted from one generation to the next by the impact of repeated suggestions ("We're a poor but proud family." "Honor thy father and mother." "Do unto others as you would have them do unto you." "In God We Trust."). Suggestions are also the basis of our belief system about ourselves. This is a mixed blessing. Since we tend to believe what we heard our parents and teachers say about us in childhood, we absorb the negative as well as the positive. ("You're a pretty girl." "You're good at sports." "You'll wind up in prison." "You'll be a drunk just like your father.").

The Coué form of positive affirmation, like the posthypnotic suggestion, tells the truth in advance by desuggesting the present condition.

Present condition, operative affirmation (present belief system): Every winter I come down with many colds.

Affirmation for change: Cold weather makes me feel especially healthy.

Present condition, operative affirmation: I don't have friends because nobody likes me.

Affirmation for change: I am an extremely likable person and have dozens of friends.

All this may sound very simplistic, and indeed it is. The fact is that our actions are very often intended to justify our belief system. Maxwell Maltz tells the story of a competent salesman who made $5,000 per annum. (Yes, not so long ago $5,000 a year was a respectable income!) He was moved to a much better territory but generated the same sales. Moved again to a difficult territory, he ended up with the same $5,000. He *saw* himself as a $5,000 salesman and, regardless of the market potential, stayed in this range. In order to improve, he first had to change what he believed about himself. Affirmations are an excellent tool for doing so.

SUGGESTIONS VERSUS AFFIRMATIONS

Affirmations have a number of characteristics in common with posthypnotic suggestion and differ in some respects.

Even more than suggestions, affirmations are like catchy commercials. They attempt to sell you the new product (your future behavior or attitude), which is far superior to your current "brand X" (your present behavior or attitude). Like good commercials they are brief, specific, hard-hitting, and often exaggerated. Their appeal is mainly to your emotions rather than to your intellect.

Unlike suggestions, they are usually phrased in the first person ("I am always full of energy."). Some writers think it is of great benefit to use the second and third person as well and include your name:

> I, John, always sleep like a log.
>
> You, John, always sleep like a log.
>
> John always sleeps like a log.

Affirmations, like suggestions, should be positive and usually in the present tense.

WRONG: I will not have headaches when I wake up in the morning.
RIGHT: When I wake up in the morning, my head is always clear.

HOW AND WHEN TO USE AFFIRMATIONS

Affirmations can be used anytime, anywhere, and in every conceivable fashion. Again, they resemble commercials in this respect. The message repeats itself endlessly. Sometimes you are conscious of it; at other times you barely listen. But there it is again and again. For example, "I am a punctual person" could be used by someone who is always late. Then, one day, when he is going to be late for his appointment, the message flashes in his head: "I am a punctual person." Punctual people are always on time. And, lo and behold, he *is* on time. He has "bought" the new product!

You can write affirmations on cards and carry them with you, paste them on mirrors, copy or type them over and over, repeat them endlessly as you drive. It is a saturation approach.

INTEGRATING AFFIRMATIONS INTO SELF-HYPNOSIS EXERCISES

You can use affirmation within the self-hypnosis sessions in the following manner. Let's assume that you're working on three subjects: losing weight, learning and understanding the stock market, and obtaining a promotion. You could use these or similar affirmations:

> By Christmas my waistline is thirty-one inches.

> I invest successfully because of my profound understanding of the market.
>
> I am an outstanding worker, and promotion follows promotion.

You can start and end your self-hypnosis tape with the above three affirmations by reciting them like articles of faith. (As they should be!) On the tape, after the induction that puts you in a state of hypnosis, you will say:

> And now, repeat after me the affirmation for this month: First, by Christmas my waistline is thirty-one inches. Second, ...

Later, when you make the suggestions themselves, you explain why the loss of weight is desirable, what the benefits will be, and how this will be achieved.

Using the same affirmation throughout the day enhances the self-hypnosis session. It will help greatly if, while you repeat the affirmation, you can also visualize the outcome—for instance, wearing pants with a thirty-one inch waist. (Don't get carried away and work on too many affirmations at one time. Use the same number of affirmations as the suggestions you're working on.)

Affirmations lend themselves to more elaborate work. If the subject interests you, read *The Psychology of Success Bulletin*, Vol. I, No. 6, November 1982.[1]

SAMPLE AFFIRMATIONS FOR FINANCIAL WELL-BEING

> I always pay cash for whatever I buy.
>
> I impress interviewers as a wise, competent, and charming person.
>
> I earn a good living by doing my own thing.
>
> My business ideas are unique and innovative.
>
> All my investments are based on thorough research.

[1]Published by the Exploration Institute, 1711-A Grove Street, Berkeley, CA 94709.

IN CONCLUSION

Be patient with your progress in your self-hypnosis program. It may take a few sessions before you get everything right. Don't expect earth-shaking changes in yourself overnight. Self-hypnosis is a *gradual* process.

Above all, don't evaluate or grade your success in practicing self-hypnosis. Consider each session a success; suggest to yourself that the next one will be even more successful.

chapter eleven

A READING GUIDE

A READING PROGRAM

Being knowledgeable about matters concerning our financial well-being requires constant updating of the facts. What was true a year ago may be as stale today as last year's newspaper. There are also few definitive works in this area; many books recommend opposing approaches, and readers must make up their own minds.

For these reasons I've decided to write a reader's guide to information rather than a reading list. This is the *beginning* of your reading program. One source will direct you to another until you are able to chart your own course. Many of the subjects mentioned here are taught in adult education programs, which are another source of information.

GENERAL READING

There are two periodicals worth reading on an ongoing basis. Practically all subjects raised in this book are discussed from time to time in the monthly magazine:

Changing Times: The Kipplinger Magazine (Editors Park, MD 20782)

The articles are written clearly and concisely. They contain all the information you'll need if you're new to the subject; if you are conversant with the subject, the articles will serve as a refresher course.

Many people—unfortunately including professionals—are oblivious to the fact that seemingly unrelated economic events are often intertwined. For example, if the wheat harvest in the USSR is poor, will the price of gold go up or down? It may go down. Russia, the second largest gold producer, will sell gold to raise cash for importing wheat.

A publication that covers all aspects of the economy and provides an ongoing business education is on the newsstands daily:

The Wall Street Journal

Whether you agree or disagree with its editorial policy, you'll probably enjoy the astonishing diversity of its long and well-researched daily feature articles. In a recent five-day period these articles dealt with falconry, forestry in Manhattan, the Day of the Dead in Manila, the story of a Lebanese town, and whether the house fly is the victim of a smear.

A general education about money manners, which may serve as a starting point, can be gotten from:

Sylvia Porter's Money Book for the '80s (New York: Avon Books, 1980)

INVESTMENT INFORMATION

I cannot, in good conscience, recommend specific investment books. Each author takes a different approach. Some of the doomsday writers, who often make the best-seller list, sound completely wacky. (Sad to say, one day I will probably regret not having followed their strange advice!)

It is my suggestion that you read as many books as you can. Some good and sound advice tends to repeat itself in many of these books (such as "Never put all your eggs in one basket"), and the specific policy that appeals to you most will emerge slowly through your diverse reading.

What may happen to you is that you'll opt for a blend of a number of approaches. This guarantees you that you won't be wiped out and almost assures you that you'll never make a real killing. Many of the more conservative writers suggest just such an approach. Since the late 1970s, for instance, they have recommended, in their model portfolios, owning *some* gold. The assumption behind this strategy is that nobody knows anything for sure. Some day you'll be happy that you have at least some gold. Conversely, if the price of gold does not go up spectacularly, you'll be glad you have only a little of the stuff.

Make it a point never to invest in anything at all just on a tip, regardless of the credentials of that tip. Anybody soliciting investment funds from the public *must* publish a prospectus. Stockbrokers usually also have these prospectuses on hand.

All companies listed on the New York or American Stock Exchanges and many other over-the-counter companies are described in informational sheets published by:

Standard & Poor

These sheets are available from brokers and large public libraries. The information is constantly updated and includes all pertinent details and evaluations. Many carry a rating, which grades the company. Brokers often publish their own research reports on a company or an industry.

Mutual funds will send you an endless stream of information about their funds. One book has all the information you need about funds in general and specific funds:

Weisenberger Investment Companies Service

It is a very costly book (close to $200 as of this writing), so ask for it in a large public library. Acquaint yourself immediately with the various types of funds; learn especially the difference between a load and a no-load fund. (The topic is discussed in great detail in the book.)

If you can't get hold of *Weisenberger,* you may start with either of these books:

Donoghue's Mutual Funds Almanac (Box 540, Holliston, MA 01746)

No-Load Mutual Fund Annual Directory (Valley Forge, PA 19481)

Just as one can write an investment book and suggest that readers invest in mothballs to protect themselves against inflation, one may distribute an investment bulletin based on the reading of tea leaves. The good investment letters feature thorough research. The bad ones serve as a soap box for the writer's cause. What they all have in common is the high subscription price. See whether you can find them in a broker's office or a public library.[1]

TAXES

If you read *Changing Times* regularly, you'll be well-informed about changes in the tax laws that affect you. What is essential for you to have on hand is a reference that will let you check on a specific question and come up with the correct answer.

Your Income Tax, by J. K. Lasser (Published yearly by Simon & Schuster)

is an inexpensive, complete guide. It is written in plain language and has a lot of hypothetical cases to clarify the practical applications of the law. It is well indexed and much easier to understand than the IRS publications. It also lists every conceivable deduction a taxpayer may be entitled to take.

[1]For a full discussion and evaluation of investment letters, see *Changing Times,* December 1982, pp. 38-41.

CAREER CHANGES

What you need more than anything else, if you don't know what you want to do with the rest of your life, are ideas to help you fertilize your thinking—something that will show you that successful biology teachers can become vice-principals or ... beekeepers!

Let me name three such works:

Where Do I Go from Here? by John C. Crystal and Richard N. Bolles (Berkeley, CA: Super Press, 1974)

What Color Is Your Parachute? by Richard N. Bolles (Berkeley, CA: Ten Speed Press, 1972)

The Three Boxes of Life, by Richard N. Bolles (Berkeley, CA: Ten Speed Press, 1978)

Once you have decided on a change, it is vital to interview people who work in the field you've chosen. If you want to open a little mom-and-pop grocery in San Francisco, you'll find out from practicing grocers that your major concern will be trigger-happy robbers. Some grocers walk around with bulletproof vests. This is the type of information you *do not* get from the Chamber of Commerce.

For a novel approach to landing a job—especially in your written communications to prospective employers—read

Executive Jobs Unlimited, by Carl R. Boll (New York: Macmillan, 1979)

Make sure you obtain the revised 1979 edition.

PURCHASING

Some people seem to be naturally more savvy about purchasing whatever they need than others. If you feel that you want to be on top of things and really know which detergent is a better buy for your money or which car has the best resale value, consult

Consumer Reports

This monthly publication is available on newsstands and libraries.

MAKING MORE MONEY

I want to insert a warning here. You might have gotten the feeling that I suggest that all readers who want to make a lot of money should give up their salaried jobs and start their own business. Let me clarify this point. Some people go into business regardless of economic considerations. They want, above all, to be their own boss. They often have to put up with a lot more aggravations than salaried workers. Considering the hours they put into the business, they get paid less than had they drawn a salary.

Other people want to go into business because they want to make more money or because it is the only way they can enjoy their working careers. In their case the business must relate to their general experience or interests if they are to enjoy the responsibility that comes with it.

I tell you this so that you don't stumble blindly into a franchise deal. You see ads that promise you that for $20,000 ($2,000 down), you'll be able to own a lemonade stand that will gross $200,000 annually. Best of all, you need no previous experience. There is ample literature on buying a franchise. Make sure you read it all *before* you start your negotiations. The franchise companies use very, very hard-selling techniques. Then, *before* you sign *anything,* interview as many franchisees as you can. Each company is different!

For information about business in general and specific ventures, get the publication list of the

Small Business Administration

They have offices in large and medium-sized cities. (Incidentally, you may qualify for a loan through this federal agency.)

For a better understanding of how you relate to money and money making, read

Money Madness: The Psychology of Saving, Spending, Loving, and Hating Money, by Herb Goldberg and Robert T. Lewis (New York: The American Library, 1979)

MOTIVATIONAL BOOKS

I have mentioned elsewhere in this work the books of Napoleon Hill and Maxwell Maltz. These books bear repeating here:

Think and Grow Rich, by Napoleon Hill (New York: Fawcett, 1979)

You Can Work Your Own Miracles, by Napoleon Hill (New York: Fawcett, 1978)

Psycho-Cybernetics: The New Way to a Successful Life, by Maxwell Maltz, M.D. (Englewood Cliffs, NJ: Prentice-Hall, 1960)

Magic Power of Self-Image Psychology: The New Way to a Bright Full Life, by Maxwell Maltz, M.D. (Englewood Cliffs, NJ: Prentice-Hall, 1964)

HYPNOSIS

We come now to literature pertaining to self-hypnosis. Learning how to hypnotize yourself is quite easy. What you want to know about are the many applications of self-hypnosis.

Hypnosis has always suffered from a bad press. It started with Anton Mesmer at the end of the eighteenth century and haunts the field to this very day. There is also a difference of opinion between believers in the "state of hypnosis" and scholars who doubt that such a separate state exists. As a result, some writers in the field of hypnosis use different nouns to describe the same phenomenon. You may pick up a book or a tape with a different title and find out that it is the same as what you have been practicing under self-hypnosis. Don't worry about titles! Also, don't worry about combining techniques of different schools and systems.

I know that by saying this I'm exposing myself to the wrath of the followers of this or that cult or doctrine. What you want to do is enter into a relaxed, focused state and, in this state, do your suggestive work. Whichever technique helps you to achieve your goal is a step in the right direction.

A lot of hypnosis books deal with physical and psychological well-being:

> *Healing with Mind Power,* by Richard Shames, M.D., and Chuck Sterin (Emmaus, PA: Rodale Press, 1978; if not available in bookstores, order directly from the publisher)

This book has many useful approaches for using self-hypnosis as a tool for health improvement and habit control. The section on self-hypnosis techniques and suggestions is very good. It is published by the Rodale Press, which is heavily involved in nutrition magazines. As a result, the book has a holistic-living section (which may not interest every reader).

> *Selective Awareness,* by Peter H. C. Mutke, M.D. (Westwood Publishing Co., 312 Riverdale, Glendale, CA 94705; if not available in bookstores, order directly from the publisher)

This is a do-it-yourself book. By regressing oneself to the origin of a physical or emotional trauma, one may get rid of the condition in the present. The techniques are useful, though the author's approach is somewhat simplistic.

Autogenic training is a kissing cousin of hypnosis. I have found it very useful with students who have difficulties in entering into a proper hypnotic state.

> *Autogenic Training Tape,* by Vera Fryling, M.D. (2510 Webster Street, Berkeley, CA 94705)

The tape teaches the listener to send healing messages to various parts of the body.

Clinical Hypnotherapy, by David Cheek, M.D., and Leslie M. Le Cron (New York: Grune & Stratton, 1968)

This is a good all-around book describing how certain emotional and physical conditions can be dealt with through hypnotherapy.

Hypnosis can be very effective in helping one cope with pain. There is a definitive work on the subject,[2] but unfortunately it was not written as a how-to book. It is also dated, because it was published before the discovery of endorphins. (These are "natural morphines" created by our own nervous system to help us cope with pain.) You can gain some knowledge about this subject by reading:

Free Yourself From Pain, by David Bresler, M.D., with Richard Trubo (New York: Simon & Schuster, 1979)

David Bresler is the director of the UCLA Pain Control Unit. Throughout the book he discusses extensively guided imagery, and he also has a section on hypnosis.

OTHER AREAS THAT USE SELF-HYPNOSIS

There are hundreds of self-hypnosis tapes on the market. They deal with subjects ranging from nail biting to successful selling. I think that by now you can make your own tapes in whatever area is of importance to you. However, if you want to sample what is commercially available, write to either address for a tape catalog:

Westwood Publishing Co., 312 Riverdale Drive, Glendale, CA 91204

Tapes, by Emmett E. Miller, M.D., P. O. Box W, Stanford, CA 94305

As I have stated a number of times throughout this book, hypnosis is a tool for change. It is not meant only for major physical and behavioral problems.

[2]Ernst R. Hilgard and Josephine R. Hilgard, *Hypnosis in the Relief of Pain* (Los Altos, CA: William Kaufmann, 1975).

Hypnosis with Friends and Lovers, by Freda Morris (San Francisco: Harper & Row, 1979)

This book is an excellent example of how self-hypnosis can be used to enrich one's life in any given area.

The Act of Will, by Roberto Assagioli (New York: Viking, 1973)

Though using a completely different label, Assagioli's method combines visualization and self-hypnosis techniques. Many readers using his methods find them very useful.

VISUALIZATION TECHNIQUES

The most comprehensive book on all aspects of visualization is

Seeing with the Mind's Eye: The History, Techniques, and Uses of Visualization, by Mike Samuels, M.D., and Nancy Samuels (New York: Random House, 1975)

It is a beautifully illustrated book and features a comprehensive reading list. There are exercises for readers who have difficulties in visualizing.

Visualizing: Directing the Movies of Your Mind, by Adelaide Bry (New York: Harper & Row, 1979)

This book contains practical exercises and techniques in this field.

Marquette University and the Institute for the Advancement of Human Behavior have been offering numerous seminars throughout the country under the title

"The Power of Imagination: Uses of Imagery in the Healing Arts"

Some of the speakers are the same in all conferences; others change with each event. Many of the speakers are physicians. The seminar I attended in San Francisco in 1982 was very interesting but, in my opinion, had one shortcoming: It was too academically oriented. If the topic is of interest to you, write for information to Marquette University, Division of Continuing Education, 1217 W. Wisconsin Avenue, Milwaukee, WI 53233.

INTUITION

Awakening Intuition, by Frances E. Vaughan (Garden City, NY: Anchor Press/Doubleday, 1979)

This book has a section on imagery and intuition that might be of interest to some readers. Intuition in business undertakings is also discussed.

YOU'RE ON YOUR OWN

Please regard everything you have read in this book as my *suggestions* to enhance your financial well-being. Some you'll accept; others you may reject. It is merely a *start*. From here on, use your own ingenuity, your own insight, your own intuition, to further your state of financial well-being.

So, begin practicing the exercises, read a few books, and start putting your subconscious to work for you. Good luck!

chapter twelve

THE SELF-HYPNOSIS TAPES

When I work with clients to help them quit smoking, the first thing I ask them in a state of hypnosis is whether they want to give up the habit. Often their answers, when hypnotized, differ from what they told me when they spoke to me in a state of ordinary consciousness.

I give this example because your reaction to the script while recording it in an "unhypnotized" state is likely to be very different from what you will experience once you are in a state of hypnosis. *Consciously* expect this difference in reactions. What matters in this case are your subconscious feelings when listening to the tape, not your intellectual evaluation of the text.

RECORDING YOUR TAPES

Before you start recording, please note the following. When you see a series of three dots (. . .), stop for a few seconds; when a longer pause is required, the number of seconds of silence is indicated by a number in parentheses. Don't worry about the exact count. If in doubt, the longer the pause, the better. Pauses give you enough time for brief reflection and also allow you to move deeper into the hypnotic state. If you need more time, stop the recorder, as discussed in Chapter 9.

Remember that tapes have leaders. Let the tape run for thirty seconds before you start recording.

Speak slowly and clearly.

STANDARD INDUCTION

You can use this induction for all the self-hypnosis exercises or alternate it or replace it with either of the alternative versions. If you erase an exercise, keep the induction portion so you won't have to rerecord it.

Yawn deeply three times ... (20)

Now close your eyes ... With your eyes closed, look up as if you're trying to see your eyebrows ...

Now let your eyes rest and start relaxing the small muscles around your eyes ... Relax them completely ... They're so easy to relax ... More and more relaxed ... Letting go of all your tensions ... Feeling the heaviness of your eyelids ... They're so heavy and relaxed that they feel as if they wouldn't work even if you wanted them to ... (15)

Now start pretending that your eyelids are glued together ... That they are stuck shut ... That there is no way you can open your eyes ... (15) Continue relaxing your eyes and pretending—pretending that you can't open your eyes and relaxing the muscles even more ... (15)

While you are pretending, gently—very gently—test your eyes. You will see that if you're pretending properly, your eyes are indeed stuck shut. Your eyelids are glued together.

Now forget all about your eyes, but let the muscles around them become even more relaxed ... (15)

Imagine yourself sitting in a wooden tub full of pleasantly warm water. There is an essence of pine in the water, and you can smell the strong, clean pine smell ... Only your head is sticking out, and you can feel moisture on your face. The water is so pleasantly warm, so soothing ... You begin to feel a little drowsy, a pleasant, floating sensation ... (20)

Gently, ever so gently, you drift deeply into a feeling of great comfort and peace ... (15) Deeper and deeper ... Letting go ... Letting go ... Feeling the warmth of the water go all through you ... (15)

If you listen carefully, you might be able to hear in the distance the soft sound of a flute ... Somebody's playing it so softly you can barely hear it. Listen ... (10)

A sense of tiredness, heaviness, laziness takes you very deeply into total relaxation ... The warm water is so soothing, and even though you are tired you can hear and understand everything ... (15)

Now, as I count backward from 10 to 1, with each number you'll go even deeper ... 10, 9, 8 ... letting go ... 7, 6, 5 ... going deeper and deeper ... 4, 3 ... more and more relaxed ... 2 ... 1 ... (15)

ALTERNATIVE INDUCTIONS

The hot-tub induction is kinesthetic; practically all readers will be able to use it. But to give you a choice of inductions, here are two more. The first is mainly visual. If you are a visual person, you can use any number of esthetically pleasing scenes. Waterfalls, snowflakes, or raindrops can serve the same purpose as the ocean in the first alternative.

The second alternative induction is intended to cause mental confusion by distorting time. Apparently when the mind can't cope readily with confusing input, it escapes into a subconscious mode. The theme for the second induction is from Herman Hesse's *Siddhartha*.

Be imaginative in composing your inductions. Combine as many elements as you can (motion, vision, touch, sound, smell, feeling). Remember: A good induction is one that works best for you.

Visual Induction

Yawn deeply three times ... (20)

Now close your eyes ... With your eyes closed, look up as if you're trying to see your eyebrows ...

Now let your eyes rest and start relaxing the small muscles around your eyes ... Relax them completely ... they're so easy to relax ... More and more relaxed ... Letting go of all your tensions ... Feel the heaviness of your eyelids ... They're so heavy and relaxed that they feel as if they wouldn't work even if you wanted them to ... (15)

Now start pretending that your eyelids are glued together ... That they are stuck shut ... That there is no way you can open your eyes ... (15) Continue relaxing your eyes and pretending—pretending that you can't open your eyes and relaxing the muscles even more ... (15)

While you are pretending, gently—very gently—test your eyes. You will see that if you're pretending properly, your eyes are indeed stuck shut. Your eyelids are glued together.

Now forget all about your eyes, but let the muscles around them become even more relaxed ... (15)

You are sitting on a very beautiful beach, looking toward the ocean. It's a perfect day, not too hot and not too cold. The sun feels pleasantly warm; your fingers are playing in the soft sand ... There's moisture on your face ... You can smell the saltiness of the slight breeze ... Listen to the sound of the surf ...

As you look at the green-blue ocean you become very peaceful and relaxed ... You're feeling somewhat heavy and drowsy ... Letting go ... Letting go ... (15)

Now look at the waves. Focus on the whitecaps ... With each wave you're going deeper and deeper. Endlessly the waves keep coming in ... Wave after wave after wave ... You feel yourself going deeper ... Still deeper ...

Count the waves as they come in ... 1 ... 2 ... 3 ... 4 ... 5 ... so many waves to count ... They keep coming in and going out ... coming in and going out ... (15)

And now your eyes become blurry and you feel so tired that you lie back on the warm sand. Your mind is at peace, and you feel very sleepy—yet you listen carefully to useful and helpful suggestions ...

Confusion Induction

Yawn deeply three times ... (20)

Now close your eyes ... With your eyes closed, look up as if you're trying to see your eyebrows ...

Now let your eyes rest and start relaxing the small muscles around your eyes ... Relax them completely ... They're so easy to relax ... More and more relaxed ... Letting go of all your tensions ... Feel the heaviness of your eyelids ... They're so heavy and relaxed that they feel as if they wouldn't work even if you wanted them to ... (15)

Now start pretending that your eyelids are glued together ... That they are stuck shut ... That there is no way you can open your eyes ... (15) Continue relaxing your eyes and pretending—pretending that you can't open your eyes and relaxing the muscles even more ... (15)

While you are pretending, gently—very gently—test your eyes. You will see that if you're pretending properly, your eyes are indeed stuck shut. Your eyelids are glued together.

Now forget all about your eyes, but let the muscles around them become even more relaxed ... (15)

See yourself walking down a gently sloping hill on a narrow path toward a lake. To your right are tall pine trees ... You can smell the strong pine fragrance ... And to your left is a swiftly flowing river ... Listen to the sound of the water as it cascades over the rocks ... (15)

As you are looking toward the river you start thinking of yourself as a river ... A river has no beginning and no end ... It flows on and on ... The past and the present merge to become the future ... And yet the future is a part of the past ... The river is made up of billions of drops, yet each drop is the river ... Keep watching the river ... How is it that something has no beginning and no end? ...

You keep walking downhill watching the river, letting go more and more ... Like the river, you are part of the past and the future, yet you are in the present ... How strange ...

Walking toward the lake and looking at the river, you are feeling very, very heavy and lazy, as you are going deeper and deeper into a state of perfect relaxation ... Keep looking at the river ... (5)

Now you are at the lake. Find a rock overlooking the blue water. The sun is so pleasant, and you feel drowsy and confused. The rock is warm, and as you're lying on it you feel so weary, so sleepy, yet your mind is open to useful and helpful suggestions ... (15)

SUGGESTIONS FOR SLEEPING SOUNDLY

Each exercise ends with the suggestion that when you come out of the state of hypnosis you'll be wide awake and full of energy. If you want to practice before you fall asleep, you need to change this suggestion. Change the *last* paragraph of each exercise, using the following text:

In a moment I will ask you to stop the recorder. This will be your cue to start drifting into a peaceful, restful, uninterrupted sleep. You will sleep soundly until tomorrow morning. You will awaken exactly when you need to wake up and will feel rested and refreshed ... Recall a time when you were a young child and you went to bed in the evening and the next thing you knew it was morning ... (10) Tonight you will sleep like this once again ... In the morning you will remember your dreams ... You are getting very drowsy, very sleepy ... so sleepy ... rest well ... stop the recorder now.

SELF-HYPNOSIS EXERCISE FOR CHAPTER THREE

Now that you're in a very relaxed, peaceful state, it's a good time for you to take stock of your financial situation ... For now, just note the information you're receiving and file it for futher study ...

There is nothing you need to do right now. Nothing to decide ...

Imagine yourself sitting in front of a large TV screen. The picture is three-dimensional. You can hear what you need to hear, and you can feel within yourself everything that's taking place on the screen. Now visualize a typical day of your working life, and concentrate on one moment of that day, a moment that sums up what your day is all about. Visualize it very clearly ... (20)

Become aware of how you're feeling as you continue to visualize ... (15)

Are you happy or sad? Interested or bored? Are there other feelings? ... (15) Focus on these feelings ... (15)

Now imagine you have the authority to change anything you wish about your working conditions: A different shift; a move to another department; working with another group of people; changing supervisors; whatever ... (15)

How do you feel now? ... (15)

Now let go of this visualization. Imagine that you're taking inventory of all your property and belongings—whatever belongs to you and your family. Survey your home ... (10) Look at the furniture; ... the clothing, ... the linen in the closet, ... the kitchen utensils, ... the books, ... the records, ... the gadgets, ... the appliances ... (15)

Do you own a lot of things? ... Are you happy with what you have? ... Do you have too little? ... Too much? ... Do you own a lot of useless stuff? ... Do you have what you really need? ... Do you shop wisely? ... Do you spend money foolishly? ...

How do you feel about your home? ... Is it the right place at the right price? ... How do you like your car? ... How do you feel riding in it? ... Some people give their cars names. What would you call yours? ...

Is there something you would really like to have right now but don't have the funds to buy? ... (15) Pretend you have acquired it ... Look at it ... Admire it ... Use it ... How do you feel now that you have it? ... Do you still want it? ... (15)

Now let go of this visualization and get in touch with how much money you have. Are you very wealthy? ... Rich? ... Well-off? ... Comfortable? ... Just getting by? ... Poor? ... Get in touch with this feeling ... (15)

Are you saving as much as you want to? ... (15) Are you in debt? ... Visualize your debts like weights that you have to carry ... How much do they weigh? ... Five pounds? Ten? Twenty-five? Fifty? ... Can you manage? ...

How do you feel about your financial situation? ... (15) If there were one change you could make right now, what would you do? ... (15)

Imagine you have all the money you want. Do you know how to manage it? ... (15) Do you know how to invest it? ... (15) See yourself talking to your bank manager or your stockbroker about your financial affairs. Do you understand what he is talking about? Does he understand you? ... (15)

Now let go of this visualization ... Imagine yourself making your living and spending your days doing something you really would like to do ... Earning all the money you need ... Owning whatever you want ... Imagine a few typical minutes of your day in this state ... Visualize yourself in the morning, the afternoon, and the evening ... (30) How do you feel? ... Are you ecstatic? ... Happy? ... Content? ... Dissatisfied? ... Is there something missing? ... What is it? ...

Now I am going to be quiet for a minute while you are assessing your state of financial well-being ... (60)

Finish your assessment as best you can ... (10) If need be, come back to it later ... Next time, when you listen to the tape, you will be able to go deeper, much deeper ... When I count to 10, your eyes will be open, you will be wide awake, and you will be in a good mood, full of energy ... 1, 2, 3, 4, 5 ... When I reach 10, your eyes will open and you'll be full of energy ... 6, 7, 8, 9, 10. Eyes open. Wide awake. Feeling fine.

SELF-HYPNOSIS EXERCISE FOR CHAPTER FOUR

Imagine that you're a film producer. You are sitting in a comfortable chair. To your right and to your left are huge screens. On the right screen you can play movies of your past and present. On the left one you can project any scene you imagine. The movies have color and sound and also convey emotions, feelings, and body sensations. Right in front of you is a computer that has all the answers you will need. Sometimes the program is complicated, and it might take a few days for the information to be processed.

Now lean back in your seat. As I count from 5 to 1, you become more and more relaxed. 5, 4, 3, 2, 1. Deeper and deeper ...

Now begin playing selected scenes of your various jobs or occupations. Just the highlights ... You might want to stop the projector to view carefully something important: a major achievement, an important promotion, being fired, whatever ... (15)

Now focus on your present job or occupation. Run through a typical day ... (15) Do you like what you see? ... Is your job important? ... To whom? ... Are you utilizing all your skills? ... Are you proud of your work? ... Is it interesting? ...

Imagine that you're being evaluated by your supervisor or your clients. What do they think of you? ... (10) What are the good things they say about you? ... (10) The bad things? ... (10) Do you agree with their evaluation? ... (10) Now evaluate yourself ... (15) How can you improve your job performance? ... (15) Do you want to do so? ... (15) Do you think you're underqualified, overqualified, or just right for the job? ... (15) If you could decide how much people doing your kind of work should be paid, how much would you pay yourself? ... (10)

Now look at the left screen. Make some adjustments in your job—a different department, another group of coworkers, a promotion, more pay, whatever ... (20) Do these changes make the job *much* better? ... (15) Of all these changes, focus on one that would make you immediately more satisfied with the job ... (15) Now ask the computer to figure out how this can be done ... Be patient, the answer will come to you ...

Now project on the left screen something you would *really* like to do, something you would consider important, meaningful, pleasant ... (15) Forget for a moment any practical aspects. Just enjoy the visualization. Run slowly through a typical day ... (15) Are you happy with this occupation? ... (15) Is it interesting? ... Do you feel you're doing something important? ... Would you want to do this sort of work for the next ten years? ... (15)

Now turn to the computer and program it to come up with answers to the following questions: First, what would it take to make this visualization come true? ... (15) Even if it is very difficult, is there some way to bring this about? ... (15) Second, if this is not feasible, is there a *similar* occupation that you can do? ... (15) Third, if even this is not feasible, what can you do to make your working life more rewarding to you? ... (15)

Later on, when you come back to the here and now and the information from the computer becomes available to you, write it down. It will probably arrive in bits and pieces. Be patient. It will all fall together ...

Every major change has to start somewhere—one step at a time. What can *you* do to improve your present conditions *now*? ... (15) Are you ready to put some effort into it by, for instance, acquiring a new skill? ... (15) Changing your attitude toward something or someone at work? ... (15) Whatever it is, focus on it ... Visualize how things will go for you after you have taken this step ... (15) Decide when and how you're going to do it ... (15)

Now project onto the left screen how things will change for you and where you will be one year from now ... (20) The more you visualize this scene, the more likely it is to come true.

Next time, when you listen to the tape, you'll be able to go deeper, much deeper. When I count to 10, your eyes will be open; you will be awake and in a good mood, full of energy. 1, 2, 3, 4, 5 ... more and more awake ... 6, 7, 8, 9, 10. Eyes open. Wide awake. Feeling fine.

SELF-HYPNOSIS EXERCISE FOR CHAPTER FIVE

Imagine that you're the chairman of your own purchasing commission. Each session of the commission will have on the agenda one item you wish to purchase. It's a nonroutine purchase and therefore needs the commission's authorization. The item may also be a service or other type of expense, such as a vacation trip, a study course, even plastic surgery. Visualize the other commissioners. They may be real persons or fictitious characters. As on any commission, they represent different points of view: lavish and frugal, liberal and conservative. The charter of the commission is to ensure that you obtain what you need at the best possible price and that each purchase enhances in some way the quality of your life. Call the commission to order. Visualize the item on the agenda ...

Why do you want to purchase it? ... (10)

Imagine yourself purchasing, owning, using it ... (15)

How much does it cost? ... Will there be other expenses connected with this item? ... Will the item take up much of your time? ... Can you afford the time? ... If you acquire this item right now, will you have to do without another item that is also important to you? ...

Compare these items by visualizing yourself using each of them ... (15) Which one is more important to you? ... Suppose you postpone the purchase of the item for one year; visualize yourself not having it ... (10)

Imagine yourself a year from now. Are you still happy that you acquired this item? ... Now imagine yourself ten years hence. Are you still happy that you acquired this item? ... Does the item add to your overall sense of well-being? ...

Do you want this item in order to please someone else? ... Whom? ... If so, is it worth the expense? ... (10)

Assign a weight in pounds to your total indebtedness—except your mortgage, if you have one. Make sure the weight represents the real situation. See yourself carrying the weight ... Is it easy to handle? Difficult? Impossible? ... (10) Now assign a weight to the item on the agenda if you want to buy it on credit. Can you handle the extra weight? ...

Is it the right time of year to purchase this item? Could you get it at a better price later? ... (10)

Do you have all the information you need in order to buy this item intelligently? ... Are you buying it from the right source? ...

In a moment you will be asked to stop the recorder so that the members of the commission can deliberate. If there isn't a general sense of agreement, you may want to call another meeting for a later date. In the meantime the answer will become obvious to you. STOP THE RECORDER UNTIL THE DISCUSSION IS OVER.

Now ask the commissioners to review your shopping policy. Do you shop wisely? ... Do the items you acquire add to your sense of well-being? ... (15) Do you have too much stuff? Too little? Let the commission make some recommendations in this area ... (15)

Now dismiss the commission and go deeper ... much deeper. As I count from 5 to 1, you become even more relaxed. 5, 4, 3, 2, 1.

Now visualize an item you would acquire if you had all the money you wanted. Visualize yourself using the item ... Enjoying it ... Now I suggest to you that as you are concentrating on the item, your subconscious will begin finding ways to make it possible for you to acquire this item. Every time you repeat this visualization it becomes more and more feasible ...

Take some time out to reflect on how the things you own affect your life. STOP THE RECORDER UNTIL YOU FINISH THIS PROCESS.

Next time, when you listen to the tape, you will be able to go deeper, much deeper. When I count to 10, your eyes will be open, you will be wide awake, and you will be in a good mood, full of energy. 1, 2, 3, 4, 5 ... more and more awake ... 6, 7, 8, 9, 10. Eyes open. Wide awake. Feeling fine.

SELF-HYPNOSIS EXERCISE FOR CHAPTER SIX

Imagine that you have bought a lottery ticket and you could win anywhere from ten thousand to a million dollars. Now focus on whatever you need and want to have, or to do, within the next three years ... (15) Visualize these things very clearly ... (15) Imagine yourself using or doing them ... (15) Do they make you happier? ... (15) How much would you need to win to acquire or do these things? ...

Now imagine that you are sitting in front of a computer. It has all the answers you need, and it can program itself even if it has very little input. However, some of the answers it will display immediately; others it will communicate to you later on when it has finished working out all the details.

Now type your financial goal, and the computer will display your objective or objectives for the next three years.... (15)

Now instruct the computer to program a plan for obtaining this sum of money. The display screen will probably indicate to you that the computer doesn't have enough information, and it will now ask for specific information.

Supply the computer with all the skills you have. Be thorough; include the skills you use for your hobbies as well as those you have used to earn a living ... (30)

As you're feeding in these skills, you might notice that the computer displays various minifilms showing you how these skills can be translated into extra income. It is only doing this in the areas that are not obvious to you . . . (15) Let the computer do this as long as is necessary. Do this without judgment about practicality. The computer shows you options; you may or may not consider them later. STOP THE RECORDER TILL THE PROCESS IS FINISHED.

Input all your positive qualities (like patience and accuracy) and all your negataive qualities (like anger and worry) . . . (20) Now let the computer display what people with these types of qualities do best . . . Be open-minded . . . (15)

Now type in the jobs through which you have earned most of your money . . . (20) Have the computer evaluate them in terms of practicality at this stage of your life . . . (15)

Now recall all the strange and outlandish schemes you have ever had for making extra money. Cancel the ones that might endanger your sense of well-being . . . Don't worry about practicality . . . (20) The computer might give you a preliminary evaluation, ask you for more information, or process it later on . . .

Now go deeper, much deeper . . . As I count from 5 to 1, you are letting go more and more . . . 5, 4, 3, 2, 1.

Let the computer display on the screen several scenarios to help you earn the extra income. These may be disjointed scenes that make little sense to you. Let them be there . . . (15) When you are back in the here and now, jot them down. It will all fall into place later.

Now focus again on the amount of extra income you want. Realize that there is a way for you to make this amount and that it will come to you. All you need are patience and resolution. As you repeat this exercise again and again, things are becoming clearer and clearer. Next time, when you listen to the tape, you will be able to go deeper, much deeper.

When I count to 10, you will be wide awake, full of energy and in a good mood. 1, 2, 3, 4, 5, 6, 7, 8, 9, 10. Eyes open, feeling fine.

SELF-HYPNOSIS EXERCISE FOR CHAPTER SEVEN

Imagine that you're the inspector general of your own financial department. Visualize yourself as a very serious, formal, and conservataive person. Facts and figures are what you understand best. Your task is to inspect your own financial state of affairs and make sure that it is in good order. You're also responsible to see that your assets keep increasing and that financial matters do not cause you undue worries.

Imagine that you are inspecting a treasury building, with a number of departments. As you are inspecting each department, you are being accompanied by the department head, who is explaining to you what's going on.

You always start your inspection at the emergency[1] funds department. How much money is in the fund? Will it be sufficient to support you if you lose your job? ... If you become ill? ... If there is some other emergency? ... Are the funds accessible at a moment's notice? ... Do they yield some interest? ... Since emergencies arise when one least expects them, you need to make sure the department functions smoothly. If any changes or improvements are needed, instruct the department head to do so right away. Assign a deadline for completion of the task ... (15)

Turn now to the current accounts department. Ask the department head whether there are enough funds on hand to meet your current expenses in an orderly fashion ... If you're not satisfied with the answer, make a note of it. You'll have to work on recommendations to change these matters later. You may have to come up with an extra source of income. Now check whether the bank statements are reconciled every month and whether all your funds are accounted for.... If there is money owed to you, what efforts are being made to collect it? ...

Proceed now to the savings department. Discuss with the department head the goal of the department. If the savings are for a specific purpose, how close is the department to achieving this goal? If the department can't meet its monthly quota, find out why not ... make a note of it. Are the savings invested so they yield interest? ... Now evaluate with the department head the overall goals of the department to see whether they're realistic ... (15) Make sure they don't cause undue stress ...

Now turn to the investment department. If there is no such department because there are no investments, assemble a skeleton staff that will be able to start the department later on ... You may

[1]If you are uncomfortable with the word *emergency,* use another term, such as *special*.

wish to decide now when this department will become operative ... make sure the staff develops an educational program, so when the department is operative, it will know what it has to do ...

If the department is operative, how is it doing? ... Is it making or losing money? ... Does it have a defined investment policy? ... What is this policy? ... (15) Are the people in the department knowledgeable? ... If not, recommend a reading or studying program ... When they use outside advice, does it have any merit? ... Does the department have a long-range goal? ... Does the investment policy cause stress? ... (10) Is the stress bearable? ... (10) If you feel that there is too much stress, order changes in the investment policy and set a target date ... (15) Is the staff too conservative? Too adventurous? ... (10) Order any other changes you deem necessary ... (10)

Now turn to the tax avoidance department. If there's no such department, establish one immediately. Assign the shrewdest person, with the most legalistic mind, to head it. Tell this person that there are always ways to reduce the tax bite and to embark on a research program to find such ways. If there is such a department, how strong is it on research? ... Does it consult reference books and periodicals? ... Does the department need outside consultants? ... Make sure that the department head understands that as a matter of principle you wish to pay the absolute minimum tax and that it is the department's job to find all legal means to bring this about.

Now visit the debt liquidation department. Make sure the staff there is alert. The people you want in this department should be very much like you: conservative, serious, and very accurate. Is the debt liquidation program realistic? ... Are the various debts causing undue worry? ... (15) Is the department's credit good? ... You may order a debt reduction by a certain date ... You may want to freeze usage of credit cards for a certain period ... You may even order the destruction of credit cards ... (15)

Now visit other departments that are appropriate in your case: custodial, if you own a lot of property; trust, if you manage another person's financial affairs ... whatever is necessary ... (15) STOP THE RECORDER IF NECESSARY.

Now adjourn with the department heads to the conference room. Review various items. Are you at ease with your investments? ... (15) Praise the department heads who have done well, and urge the rest to do better ... (15) Do you have a feeling that there's something you should do or not do with your finances at present? ... (15) Sum up everything, and decide what specifically is to be done over the next six months ... (15) When you come back to the here and now, put it in writing.

Next time, when you listen to the tape, you will be able to go deeper, much deeper. When I count to 10, your eyes will be open; you will be wide awake and in a good mood, full of energy. 1, 2, 3, 4, 5 ... more and more awake ... 6, 7, 8, 9, 10. Eyes open. Wide awake. Feeling fine.

SELF-HYPNOSIS EXERCISE FOR CHAPTER EIGHT[2]

Imagine that you're young, strong, and healthy. You're a competent and experienced mountain climber. Tomorrow you'll tackle a most challenging peak—a 10,000-foot summit. There, on the top of the mountain, is your goal—a test you must take, a course of studies you want to complete, a task you must perform. You'll set out at dawn, and you must complete your climb by nightfall, which symbolizes the deadline for achieving your goal.

It is dawn now, and you're starting out. You're fully equipped—good shoes, warm clothing, and enough food and water. As you're walking briskly toward the mountain, you visualize your goal clearly. Be very sure that you want to undertake the climb. It is difficult and dangerous ... (15)

The first 6,000 feet are the easiest. Just steady, steep climbing. During this part of the climb, you tackle the easiest aspects of achieving your goal, the problems that are the simplest to solve ... As you're climbing and sweating profusely, you focus on minor problems involved in achieving your goal ... (20)

Now you are passing a sign saying that the elevation is 5,000 feet. You turn and look back to where you started on your journey.

[2]If you feel uncomfortable with the mountain-climbing analogy of this exercise, feel free to substitute another difficult and dangerous activity with which you are more comfortable.

You're amazed how swiftly you have climbed this high. You look up. The remaining half of the mountain looks pretty rough, but you have confidence in yourself, and you're determined to carry on.

Now you've reached the 6,000-foot level. You sit down for your first meal and a well-deserved rest. Reviewing your progress this morning, you feel that you've done pretty well for yourself. You feel proud of yourself. It seems that your body responds to your determination and willpower, just as your mind is guided by your resolve. As long as you're determined, your body and mind will continue to work perfectly for you. You look back and recall vividly difficult achievements in your past, and you derive strength from them ... (15)

Now you're ready for the second leg of your climb, to the 9,000-foot level. This will be trickier terrain. Much of it is without a trail, and you'll have to use your arms to pull yourself up from rock to rock. You're aware that you must be extremely careful to make sure that each rock can support your weight. As you start climbing, you contemplate the more difficult aspects of achieving your goal. You examine carefully any dangers to yourself or other people that might arise from your endeavor, such as too much time or money or energy spent on this project ... whatever ... (15)

As you slowly and carefully hoist yourself up, you consider and solve fairly difficult problems related to your goal ... (15) Now you've reached the 8,000-foot level. You're drenched with sweat and your arms and legs are aching. Pretty soon you'll reach the point of no return. It's your last chance to turn back in time to reach base without being exposed to a night on the mountain. Visualize your goal once again ... If it is worth it, and you're still determined enough, go on ... (20) Now continue with renewed energy and determination ...

At the 9,000-foot level you stop for your second meal and rest. The third leg, though only 1,000 feet, is the most difficult and dangerous. The thin air and icy cold will test your strength; you'll encounter glaciers with hidden crevices. Even though you'll be short of time, you'll have to calculate each step so you don't fall into one. This time the rocks will be slippery with ice and very difficult to grasp.

Prepare yourself before starting. Put on your warmest clothing and a pair of thick gloves. Overcome your weariness and become more alert and focused mentally and physically. Visualize now all the advantages your goal will bring you ... (20) During this leg you deal with the most complicated problems of achieving your goal. With each step, mindful of the dangers, sensing the tension in your muscles and the tiredness of your body, you continue to deal effectively and carefully with the situation, no matter how difficult it appears ... (20) It seems that 1,000 feet will take 1,000 minutes to climb. But time is short and it's getting late. You're only 200 feet away from your goal. Your body is utterly exhausted, but your determination drives you on. You *will* reach the top of the mountain; you *will* achieve your goal. You visualize it once again ...

The sun is setting, and it is starting to grow dark. Utterly worn out, yet elated beyond anything you've ever experienced, you reach the top ... your goal ... (15)

You lie down on the ground, barely strong enough to look at your goal. Now the person who matters most to you reaches for your hands and pulls you up. The person is saying, "Congratulations. You have made it. You have conquered the mountain." Now you're saying to yourself, "Yes, I am a winner. I never give up. I never quit. I am proud of myself. I am strong and courageous." Every time you repeat this visualization you derive strength and determination to achieve your goal.

In a moment I am going to count to 10 and bring you back to the here and now. Concentrate now on your body and feel how strong, healthy, and youthful it is. You are feeling exceptionally healthy and well now ... (20) Next time, when you listen to this tape, you'll go deeper ... much deeper ...

When I count to 10, your eyes will be open and you will be wide awake. 1, 2, 3, 4, 5, 6, 7, 8, 9, 10. Eyes open. Wide awake. Feeling fine.

SATORI TAPES

In Chapter 9 I referred to the ninety-minute cassette tape I produced, which contains all the self-hypnosis exercises in this book. After a great deal of reflection, I named this undertaking Satori Tapes.

Satori is the essence of Zen Buddhism. I hesitated using such a lofty concept for a mere tape dealing with exercises for financial well-being. Yet the definition of *satori* is exactly what these exercises are designed to achieve. It is defined as an "intuitive looking into the nature of things in contraindication to the analytical or logical understanding" of them.[3] Satori allows one to look at things from a completely different angle so that all "opposites and contradictions are united and harmonized into a consistent organic whole."[4] I hope the exercises and the tape itself meet these noble goals.

To obtain the tape, write to Satori Tapes, 1775 Old County Road, #9, Belmont, CA 94002. Please send a check or money order for $11.95 + $1.50 for shipping and handling. (California residents please add 6% sales tax.)

For faster service, Visa and Mastercard holders can order by phone. Outside California call toll-free (800) 544-4444. In California call (415) 592-4902.

[3]William Barrett, ed., *Zen Buddhism, Selected Writings of D. T. Suzuki* (Garden City, NY: Doubleday/Anchor Books, 1956), p. 84.

[4]Ibid.

INDEX